20 LB. BY 1 OZ.
MADE IN ENGLAND
LYLES BLACK TREACLE
ABRAM LYLE & SONS
SUGAR REFINERS
454g e
LYLES GOLDEN SYRUP
ABRAM LYLE & SONS
SUGAR REFINERS
907g e
Friend

Pretty Pastel Style

Pretty Pastel Style

decorating interiors with pastel shades

Selina Lake

Words by Joanna Simmons
Photography by Catherine Gratwicke

rps
LONDON • NEW YORK

DESIGNER
Toni Kay and Lucy Gowans

EDITOR
Henrietta Heald

LOCATION RESEARCH
Selina Lake and Jess Walton

PRODUCTION MANAGER
Gordana Simakovic

ART DIRECTOR
Leslie Harrington

EDITORIAL DIRECTOR
Julia Charles

STYLING Selina Lake

First published in 2013
by Ryland Peters & Small
20–21 Jockey's Fields
London WC1R 4BW
and
519 Broadway, 5th Floor
New York, NY 10012
www.rylandpeters.com

10 9 8 7 6 5 4 3 2 1

ISBN 978-1-84975-359-3

A CIP record for this book
is available from the British Library.

Library of Congress CIP data has been applied for.

Printed and bound in China

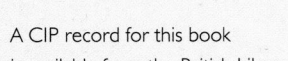

PASTIGLIE
AROMATICHE
LIMONE
DISSETANTI
LEONE
RIFIUTARE
LE
IMITAZIONI

Contents

prettyPastel
style

Introduction

Colours are moody. Colours are personal. Colours – like names or scents – carry all kinds of associations. Pastels are no exception. Hear the word 'pastel' and you may instantly imagine the sugary pink of a little girl's bedroom or the cheerful, springtime shades found on retro floral fabrics. Today, these saccharine visions are only part of the story, because pastels are enjoying an exciting, dynamic revival.

Featuring inspiring homes from around the world, *Pretty Pastel Style* illustrates the fresh direction these subtle colours are taking, from rooms painted top to bottom in layers of muted tones to understated spaces, where soft pastel hues can be found in everything from vintage china to a state-of-the-art oven.

In addition, the practicality of the pastel palette is gloriously demonstrated on every page. Pastel colours are incredibly good at warming up a room and making a small space feel bigger. They are versatile, too, evolving into something more complex and edgy when teamed with other shades, be those fresh whites and off-whites or vibrant neons.

So ditch the sludgy greys that have dominated the interior landscape in recent years and explore this appealing spectrum. The colours may be familiar, but their effects on a space are often surprising and witty. Whether you use pastels as accents or to cover large areas of wall, they bring life, interest and just a splash of humour to even the most sensible home.

Elements

Pastels make the perfect accompaniment to a white scheme. They help to punctuate its neutrality, without making too bold a statement or dominating the overall look of the space in the way that bright, saturated shades can. As shown here, pastel tones on magazine covers and book spines, in photos and on glassware create subtle pockets of interest without disturbing the tranquil feel.

Modern Pastels

Modern pastels pack an exciting, edgy punch. The palette's soft, ice-cream shades take on a fresh new feel when teamed with rich textures and contrasting accents of super-bright colour, helping them to stay the cool side of sweet. To keep the look sharp, rather than sugary, aim to create unexpected combinations.

Fashion designers regularly revisit the pastel palette, particularly for their spring and summer collections – and the catwalk can provide inspiration aplenty when decorating your home. Gentle tones of peach, bonbon yellow and cool mint look pretty without being girlie when layered together, paired with metallics or contrasted with darker tones. Working in interesting textures, from super sheers to thick denim, also does much to sharpen this colour spectrum, ensuring that it looks contemporary.

The modern pastel scheme for interiors builds on these clever catwalk ideas. Forget rooms dressed entirely in sugary shades and lacking edge; the latest approach to using pastels is far more dynamic. Soft shades are punctuated with pops of bright colour and sharpened up with statement furniture. Accents in electric blue or neon pink work particularly well against chalky pastels, but the best way to find the perfect contrast is experimentation. Often, unlikely tones sit beautifully together: hot yellow against pale green; tangerine teamed with smoky pink.

ABOVE *Vintage alarm clocks make a quirky display. Their minty pastel tones are revved up by a fourth clock in dark green. Adding a darker version of the predominant pastel is a great way to give a display some depth.*

RIGHT *Pastel pink and peachy orange are not everybody's ideal colour combination, but brought together on the bench and table in this living room, these confident shades create an exciting partnership.*

LEFT *Classic wooden chairs are given a modern makeover with a lick of pastel paint. Arranged around a table with a chunky pink top, they make a striking and witty focal point in this predominantly white space.*

RIGHT *Modern pastel schemes are kept fresh by incorporating shots of bold colour. Here, the flex on this simple light is a lush egg-yolk yellow, rather than the standard white, adding a pop of colour at ceiling height.*

BELOW RIGHT *Hot neon colours make excellent accents in a pastel scheme. They help to draw the eye to details in the room and brilliantly wake up a mellow palette. The punky personality of this yellow cabinet is enhanced by teaming it with a shocking-pink basket.*

When it comes to creating pockets of punky interest in a modern pastel room, less is more. A few notes of neon will invigorate any pastel and help to keep the mood up to date. Work it in by means of accessories or soft furnishings, or use hot, strong colour to highlight detail – perhaps a door or window frame – or to reinvent an existing piece, such as a lamp base or table top.

Pastel style also plays with intensity to achieve an up-to-date feel. Pastels vary in tone and depth just as brights or neutrals do, opening up huge design possibilities. For a softly modern scheme, keep your pastels subtle and pale, then punctuate them with a few shots of something darker. For a richer look, choose the blues, pinks or yellows you love, and use some from the pastel end of the spectrum and others from the hot, saturated side. This creates a warm, layered effect.

Think out of the box when it comes to where and how you use pastel shades. Walls are the largest surface area in any room, but a modern scheme doesn't play it safe by simply painting each one the same colour. In a bedroom, consider applying several pastel tones in broad vertical bands to give a chic panelled effect, or create a faux headboard with a rectangle of pastel paint behind the bed. Try using different pastel shades on adjacent walls or extend the colour scheme to the floor by painting boards in candy tones or laying pale-coloured rugs; to prevent pastel overkill, choose rugs with a geometric or graphic pattern.

RIGHT *This iconic Bubble Chair, designed by Eero Aarnio, has been hung in front of a bay window so the owner can relax here and gaze over the garden.*

Another innovative approach to pastels is to use them as accents in a mainly white scheme. A pink table or a chair painted dusky blue will add interest to a simple white room, without diminishing its fresh, light feel. You can also take the pastel theme in more unusual directions. Many large kitchen appliances, including refrigerators and cookers, are available in pastel shades. Or hunt down salvaged pieces. Look out for metal ceiling lights, kitchenalia or clocks, for example – any objects that combine character with colour.

When it comes to furniture, have fun creating clashes of form and feel. Modular, clean-lined furniture is softened by upholstery in dusky pink or apricot, while an austere classic such as a wingback chair suddenly looks more inviting when covered in pale blue linen. Incorporate textures, too – a sheepskin rug dyed a baby-soft pink or woodwork painted in rich gloss paint, for example.

The modern pastel look is all about creating unlikely pairings and experimenting with materials and finishes, to find new and surprising ways to bring these familiar colours into your home.

ABOVE LEFT *Modern pastel schemes often layer chalky tones for a look that has real depth. Here, minty walls are broken up with a primrose-yellow shelf and chair, while the tablecloth, with its geometric print, adds useful bite to the muted-green backdrop.*

LEFT *A fail-safe backdrop of plain white in this hallway makes a good basis for a mishmash of items in various pastel shades. Ceramics, bags, clothes and coat pegs introduce little flashes of colour, in a display that is ever changing.*

A living room in a large country house is given a touch of frivolity with a colour scheme of soft pink. Old floorboards from a French army barracks were sanded and waxed for a rustic look. They provide a strong, earthy contrast to the feminine wall colour.

Saturated shades and pale pastels make an unlikely but effective combination. Here, bright pink walls are the vivid backdrop to chairs with soft green seat pads. The overall scheme stays sophisticated, with dark floorboards, marble countertops and a crystal candelabra adding grown-up glamour.

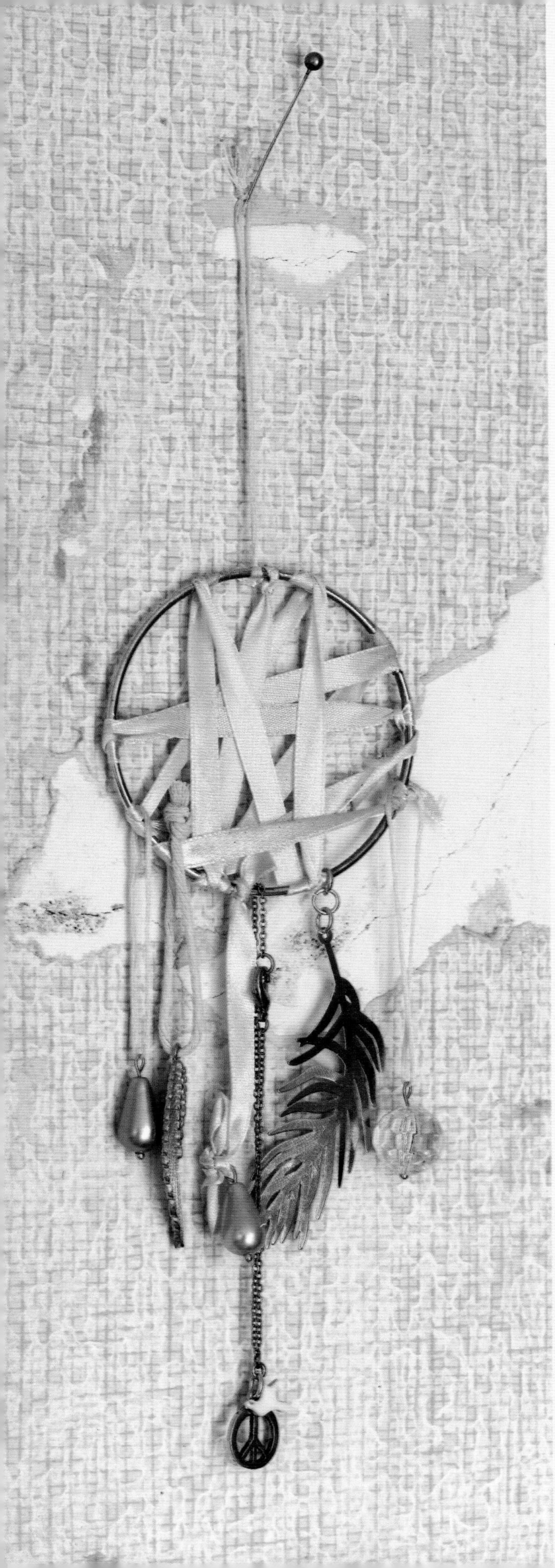

Vintage Pastels

Elegant, smoky and beautifully subtle, vintage pastels are wonderfully sophisticated. They are worlds away from the sugared-almond shades so often associated with a pastel palette. Instead, these subdued, moody schemes carry suggestions of old-world glamour – of once vivid colours that have grown muted and faded through time.

Vintage pastels are subtle and charming. They bear little resemblance to the cute candy colours also found in this colour group. Rather, the vintage pastel palette is where pinks, peaches and lilacs grow up and become sophisticated. It is crammed with hues that look as though they have aged and mellowed. Each colour hints at a long history, its muted feel making you wonder if it was once much brighter, and whether it has been bleached by the sun or softened by time.

A vintage pastel room is calm and understated. Creating this atmosphere of gentle elegance is easy, as long as you stick to the duskier, moodier end of the spectrum. Choose colours that reference interiors from centuries gone by, whether these are the pale champagne and plaster-pink shades found in a French chateau or the quiet creams and yellows of a country cottage. Many heritage paint ranges include interesting shades that can be classed as pastel, but are extremely subtle in tone and create a pleasingly flat, chalky finish.

LEFT *This pretty homemade decoration adds a pocket of detail to a rough wall of peeling paper. It is made from a bangle, with a length of soft pink ribbon woven over it. Chains and charms, taken from old necklaces, are also strung from it.*

RIGHT *A pared-down, rustic backdrop of raw plaster walls and distressed paintwork is teamed with vintage finds in pastel shades. Paintings, embroidered table linen and fine china introduce colour and pattern to the dining space, gently softening the scheme.*

In addition to using matt paint in dusky tones, you can enhance the vintage look by hanging wallpaper. Choose watery pastel shades and an elegant, rather than a graphic, pattern. The wallpaper should fade into the background, not grab your attention. Floral patterns are an obvious choice, but go for small-scale repeats instead of huge blooms. Look out for papers decorated with sprigs, buds, leaves, birds or rambling roses. These patterns will help to create a low-key, vintage backdrop.

Vintage-style fabrics are widely available – think pastel chintzes or toile de Jouy – and they are easy to work into any room. Use them simply for cushion covers or throws, or create greater impact by making curtains or upholstering furniture or footstools in a variety of old-fashioned fabrics. Look out, also, for remnants of antique linen or cotton, perhaps with hand-embroidered details, that you can transform into a tablecloth or pillow slip. Flea markets and eBay are rich hunting grounds.

Finding the right colour should be easy. The pastel tones that are appropriate to this look come as standard with vintage textiles, since the natural dyes used in the past had a more muted character, and any patterns or details may have faded over time, creating just the right weathered note.

In keeping with the knocked-back quality of the colours, the contents of a vintage pastel room should appear low key and well used. Choose furniture with a distressed finish and armchairs or sofas with faded, even frayed, upholstery. Organic, natural textiles that age beautifully, such as linen and cotton, really capture

LEFT *An upstairs hallway brims with personality thanks to a vintage-style wallpaper. Its watery background and subtle pattern make the paper design easy to live with as well as characterful.*

ABOVE RIGHT AND RIGHT *The pretty tones in these old pieces of china exemplify pastels at their sophisticated best. Creating a mismatched set is an inexpensive way to bring vintage pastel style to your dining table.*

the vintage vibe. Look out for knitted or crocheted blankets, lace work or doilies, to add to the prettiness of your vintage pastel scheme.

With a subtle pastel backdrop in place, add some interesting details to personalize the scheme. Again, flea markets are good places to track down vintage homewares, which often come ready dressed in just the right note of aged, faded pastel. Think pretty patterned teacups made from delicate china; a hand-embroidered cushion cover; a wooden stool with its pastel paintwork knocked and chipped. If you find a piece you love but the colour is wrong, consider distressing, stencilling, painting or re-covering it to create the right tone.

Finally, don't forget those easy but effective finishing touches. Fresh flowers bring instant old-world nostalgia to a vintage scheme. Choose cottage-style blooms in bleached-out tones, or indulge in old-fashioned roses, which come in gorgeously subtle shades of pink, yellow and apricot. For a lush, romantic flourish, arrange them informally in a patterned jug or a chipped teapot.

ABOVE *Gold and pastel colours are a match made in heaven. These beautiful vintage cups with their shiny interiors bring a splash of glamour to a simple stripped-wood table, and the pastel tones on their saucers look as though they were inspired by the teatime treats being served here.*

RIGHT *A simple cupboard has been given a new look with a coat of paint. The soft green harmonizes with the pastel tones in this bedroom, while new door knobs add decorative detail.*

FAR RIGHT *A lovely vintage cream on the wall softens the classic white of this traditional kitchen. It is a deliberately ambiguous, muted tone – the perfect backdrop for a painted shelf and a collection of vintage finds.*

RIGHT *The faded upholstery on a piece of second-hand or family heirloom furniture can bring vintage pastel colour into a room. The moss-green cover on this old tub chair is cleverly balanced by the brighter shades on the cushions.*

FAR RIGHT *Unfussy elegance is central to the vintage pastel look. Here, that feel is achieved with walls painted soft cream. Distressed floorboards and old industrial chairs with sturdy metal bases add some grit to the scheme.*

LEFT *This simple, bold scheme derives its style from a minimal colour palette. A vintage lampshade in a strong peach colour and bottles made of brown glass brilliantly punctuate the white background of an airy dining space. To prevent the room from appearing two tone, fresh flowers in pastel shades stand in each bottle, while some simple artwork adds contrasting pink.*

ABOVE *You might not consider using this subtle salmon shade in a living room, but this example shows how good it can look. An elegant pattern on the walls, hand-painted in green, adds gorgeous detail, and vintage wood-and-rattan chairs are softened with embroidered cushions.*

Handmade Pastels

Give your creativity a colour scheme by making pastels your first-choice palette for craft projects and handmade items. These friendly, feel-good tones are the perfect fit for easy creations such as bunting, while a pot of pastel paint can turn a wooden table into a work of art. Have fun!

ABOVE *Creative touches add interest to this spacious, comfortable living space. Soft green and pale sand colours have been used on the walls, and a similar strength of pastel, this time in a greyish-blue, brightens up the legs of the wooden table. Paper pom-poms in stronger versions of the colours used elsewhere punctuate this chalky scheme.*

Intense lime and sea-green shades have been used to make a strong statement in this hallway. The boldness of these colours has been significantly softened and made more playful by the addition of bunting sewn from patterned fabric in pastel pinks and purples.

LEFT *Painting the tongue-and-groove wall between these cabinets links the two pieces visually so that they appear more like a dresser than separate cupboards. Leaving open the sliding doors allows glimpses of the pastel china inside.*

BELOW LEFT *It is easy to reinvent second-hand wooden furniture simply by painting it. This old stool has been given striking yellow legs, then sticky-backed plastic with a lace design has been stuck on top for added interest.*

RIGHT *Hanging only a lampshade frame, rather than a finished shade, means its attractive shape can be appreciated; the addition of model birds transforms it into a mini work of art. For further personality, the flowers below have been arranged in unusual pots.*

Pastel colours are incredibly versatile. As we have already seen, teaming pastels with white for a simple look or with edgy brights for a contemporary feel transforms them, kicking their reputation for sweetness into the long grass. These shades are certainly soft, but therein lies their strength. They are easy tones to introduce into any room – a happy middle way between super-safe neutrals and strong saturated hues.

Painting walls in pastel shades or sourcing pastel furnishings or details is one way to bring these colours into your home, but crafting your own pieces is another. Whether you are skilled with a crochet hook or handy with a paintbrush, there are endless ways to personalize your space while peppering it with pastel notes.

Pastel colours are by nature fun and upbeat. They do not have the same feel as serious greys or sensible neutrals, and therefore go particularly well with certain handmade creations. Bunting is a great example. It is easy to make and looks festive and nostalgic in pretty pinks, lilacs and yellows. Look out for remnants at fabric stores or yard sales and choose strong, unabashed pastel shades that suit this jolly decoration. In addition to florals, pick up ginghams, spots and

stripes, too, in matching tones. If your skills extend to sewing, stitching a patchwork quilt or throw from pastel fabric remnants makes good use of inexpensive material and is a homespun way to work soft colour into a room. Similarly, a blanket stitched together from crochet squares in pastel shades looks wonderfully nostalgic, reminiscent of the pretty homemade baby blankets that were typically draped over prams in the past. Use a blanket like this to brighten up a neutral sofa or hide the worn upholstery on a chair arm.

A pot of pastel paint is another invaluable resource when it comes to creating a handmade scheme. Any wooden furniture, from shelves to chairs and tables, can be sanded down and painted in a mellow tone. This is more than just a satisfying way to introduce colour; it's inexpensive and eco-friendly, too.

Flea markets and yard sales are full of used wooden furniture that, once repainted, takes on a new lease of life. When out hunting for pieces, look beyond the finish and consider the form and shape. If they appeal, and the item is sound, it's ripe for a makeover.

ABOVE LEFT *A homespun project can look decorative displayed on a shelf before completion. These crochet squares are neatly stacked on a mantelpiece so that their colours can be enjoyed as they wait to be stitched together to make a blanket or throw.*

LEFT *A collection of crafting essentials has been arranged on open shelves. Balls of wool are piled into a bright basket, while rolls of spotty ribbon and swatches of patterned fabric are kept in organized stacks.*

ABOVE *Pastels featured prominently in interior design styles of the 1940s and 1950s, particularly in floral patterns of the kind that Cath Kidston has made popular again today. These tea towels and crocheted coasters strike a cheerful retro note.*

OPPOSITE *It is a common misapprehension that pastels must always look sugary. This room demonstrates how they are, in fact, easy to live with and a great way to weave understated colour into a simple scheme.*

Kate Morton
Tilbake til Riverton
SUE MONK KIDD

LEFT *A simple shelf unit provides accessible storage for craft materials in this creative corner, where everything from fabric to ribbons and sequins is kept. Paper globes in a deliciously soft pink colour are hung from the ceiling and add a witty touch.*

RIGHT *A wire lampshade frame makes an eye-catching mobile-cum-artwork. Here, crochet swatches are suspended from the frame with ribbon, but you could attach beads, pom-poms, fabric animals or felted hearts – whatever takes your fancy.*

BELOW RIGHT *A simple-to-update display of favourite photos, lists, children's artwork and cute images adorns the side of this cupboard. Using coloured tape adds a splash of colour, too, and gives the display a relaxed, informal look.*

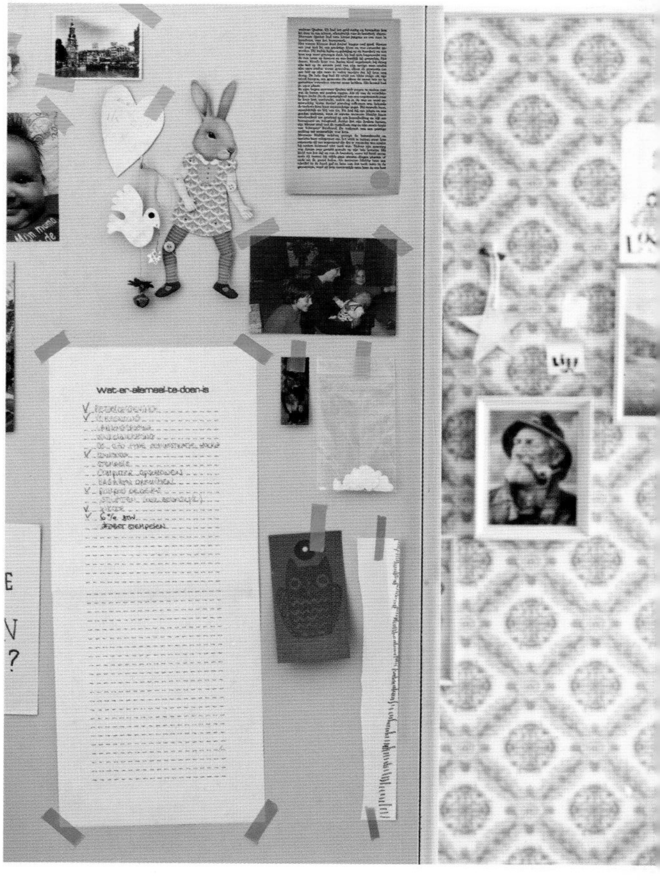

Your pastel-painted furniture can look as subtle as you like. Choose a muted shade and paint the entire piece, or pick something punchier and use it on one section – try painting only the legs of a chair or just the top of a table, for example. This approach helps to avoid pastel overkill yet still creates a pocket of colour. Play around with different finishes, too. The sheen of gloss paint will slightly emphasize and intensify a pastel shade, while a distressed finish brings the suggestion of age to wooden furniture. Advice and tutorials on how to distress furniture are available online.

When you have finished being crafty, display your materials. Stack up swatches of left-over fabric or crochet squares on open shelves so that you can enjoy their colours and patterns. Pile balls of wool into baskets or bowls, or isolate objects in a glass cloche – it's a lovely way to display anything from buttons to cotton reels. Seeing your materials together may also suggest new colour combinations or inspire your next project. Whatever the project turns out to be, remember that this is a chance to have fun and personalize your space. It's where craft and candy colours meet for a relaxed, unique take on pastel style.

M. NIJHOFF

LEFT *Creating a simple pastel scheme can be as easy as using a single pale shade to bring colour to a pure-white space. Here, the handrail on the stairs has been painted, creating a thread of green that travels up through the house.*

OPPOSITE *A pinboard crafted from thick fabric stretched over a piece of wood is home to a simple arrangement of beautiful pastel treasures. To avoid a cluttered display, a generous amount of space has been left around each object, making the individual items easier to appreciate.*

Simple Pastels

There is no need to drench your walls in sweetie shades to bring pastel style to your home. Instead, create a neutral backdrop and then introduce pastels as accents. Easy to pull off and very hard to get wrong, this is a fun, foolproof way to enjoy the soft subtlety of pastels in any room.

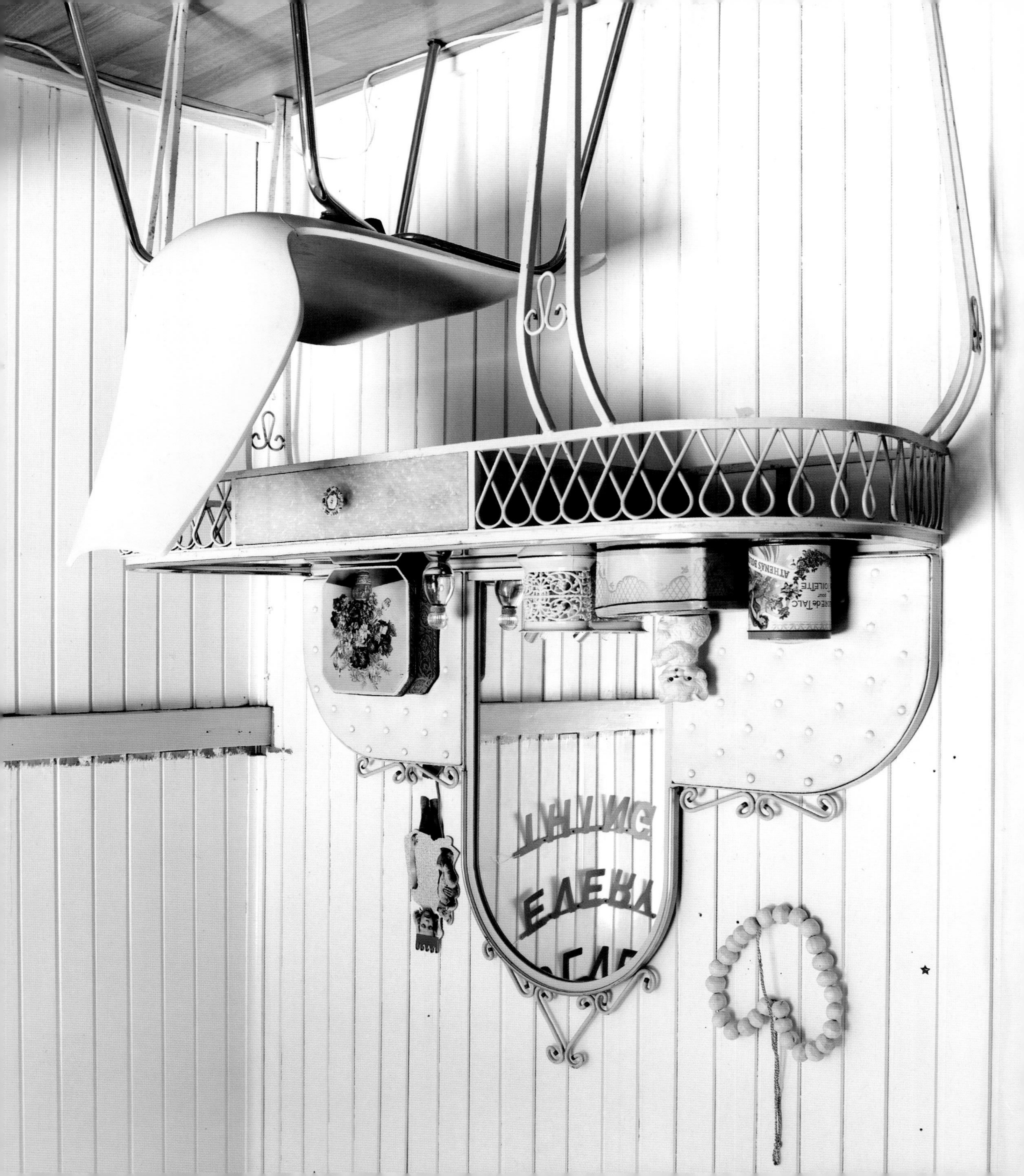

Almost any colour can work in your home when used sparingly, and pastels are no exception. So, if you thought these powdery colours weren't for you, think again. When used in moderation and set against a neutral background, their potential for sugariness is diminished and these subtle tones are shown off at their best.

The fail-safe recipe for a simple pastel scheme begins with white walls and wooden floors. Used in any room of the house, these two ingredients will create a clean backdrop for your furniture and finds. Choose pure white or explore the huge variety of off-white shades available. These hint-of-a-tint colours are wonderfully versatile, allowing you to keep the background neutral while introducing a suggestion of pastel colour. Create further interest with texture. Tongue-and-groove panelling, for example, gives a room a rustic, cabin-like feel and adds depth to a white scheme, without disrupting the fuss-free vibe. In a very dark or small room, you might like to paint floorboards white, too, to help bounce light around and increase the feeling of space.

Then all you need do is add some pastel notes. Where you introduce these is up to you, but work them in sparingly, to act as gentle accent colours. Dotted here and there, these mellow tones will lead the eye around the room, instead of shouting for attention. They also help to reduce the starkness of a white scheme, warming it up and knocking off any sterile edges, even when used in just a handful of locations.

LEFT *A simple and flexible way to bring pastels into your home is by means of small objects, rather than through walls or furniture. Here, a gorgeous antique dressing table in pale cream is home to a collection of vintage tins in faded tones.*

ABOVE RIGHT AND RIGHT *Clean white walls are the perfect backdrop for quirky finds and treasures. Vintage china, storage tins, coloured glassware and a sprig of fresh flowers are easy-to-find pastel elements that will pep up a simple scheme.*

Choosing which pastels to use is not difficult. Start by looking at objects you already own with pastel detail in them, then use that colour elsewhere, such as on a rug or a blind. You might have a much-loved teapot or lamp that can serve as the starter colour, which you can then reproduce in a few spots around the room for an understated, balanced look. Whether that shade is a dusky coral or a misty lilac, when teamed with cool white and given space to breathe, it will look delightful.

Alternatively, take inspiration from the natural world. Creating the simple pastel look can be as effortless as adding a single rose to an all-white room. It's that easy!

Take this as a starting point and build on the theme – a bigger bunch of flowers or a few stems in glass vases lining a mantelpiece will contribute soft, seductive pastel colour to a plain scheme. The wonderful advantage of adding colour with flowers is that when one bloom wilts you can replace it with another in a slightly different shade or variety.

ABOVE *A beautiful selection of decorative china, saucers and doilies is displayed on a platter. Most of the items are white, but by adding a few blooms in pastel tones and buttons in candy colours, the austerity of the white is diminished and the whole arrangement looks wonderfully elegant.*

RIGHT *Displaying china on a plate rack is a simple way to add some pastel colour to your home. It also keeps your favourite plates and platters handy and allows you to enjoy their colours and shapes when not in use.*

FAR RIGHT *These cabinet doors have a lip rather than a handle, which preserves their streamlined look. Pops of pastel colour, on the splashback, the utensils and the china, soften these sensible, functional units.*

RIGHT *White units topped by a wooden work surface is a pairing seen in kitchens around the world. Here, the addition of a colourful rug, flowers and some pastel china pieces gives real charm to a practical space.*

FAR RIGHT *White-painted walls and simple furniture receive the pastel treatment in this dining space by the use of a pink tablecloth. Green china and pretty flowers add just a pinch more pastel personality.*

Customizing old furniture is a creative and inexpensive way to splash some pastel tints around your home. Paint wooden pieces in shades you love, then add more colour by upholstering seats in vintage pastel fabric or lining cabinet doors with retro wallpaper. Scour flea markets for items ripe for a makeover, or reinvent what you already own.

Of course, you might like to use something more permanent as a means of introducing pastel tones. Again, start small and keep it simple. Experiment with pastel-coloured textiles, which are easy to move around or to alter. A throw draped over a white sofa will add colour and comfort while protecting the upholstery at the same time. Cushions, seat covers, tablecloths and place mats are other easy-to-find items that can quickly inject some pastel prettiness into your neutral scheme. Change their location within the room or around the house to keep the look fresh, or personalize them by stitching on trimmings, buttons or ribbon.

Walls are ideal locations for a sprinkling of pastels. A selection of postcards, a vintage print or a string of bunting can bring welcome colour to a white wall. In a cooking space, display pieces of pastel china on open shelves or hang floral tea towels on a peg rail. Leave your favourite pastel-coloured jug or bowl on display, and then keep work surfaces clear, for an uncluttered effect. Pastels are subtle, after all, and in a simple scheme they are best appreciated when they stand alone.

ABOVE RIGHT *The corner of this white living area is an inviting place to relax thanks to the cushions and throws in pastel colours that are arranged across the seating. Here is a wonderful example of how pastels can warm up and personalize a space.*

RIGHT *There is just a light sprinkling of pastels in this informal display – a doily and touches of pink in the artwork – but it's enough to draw the eye and add character to a large expanse of white.*

FAR RIGHT *Soothing pastels work perfectly in a bedroom. In this light, tranquil sleeping space, the pale green paint on one wall is picked up in the darker mirror frame and cushions, and contrasted with pops of hot pink and mustard yellow.*

Details

Colour palettes and patterns

If you thought pastels were girlie or frivolous, think again. This is a colour palette that is growing up. Pale, interesting and superbly versatile, pastels can work with any design style. Introduce them in bold blocks, on patterned textiles and wallpaper, or simply dotted around in the form of accessories for splashes of pretty, witty colour.

ABOVE *These crochet coasters are much more fun than most shop-bought examples. Source something similar from a craft fair, or get out your crochet hook and have a go yourself. The soft pastel colours of the yarns bring charm to a white table top.*

ABOVE *Patterned wallpaper and a retro floral tablecloth inject masses of pastel colour into this dining space, but the fun doesn't stop there. China, glasses and knives and forks with coloured handles introduce extra pastel notes.*

LEFT *You don't need to buy a lavish bouquet of flowers to bring some natural pastel colour into your home. Here, a couple of roses have been arranged in two water glasses to make a simple and elegant display.*

Like experimental works of art, pastels tend to divide opinion. We may love them or loathe them, and if it's the latter the reason may be that this colour palette comes with baggage. Pastels often conjure images of little girls' bedrooms or the Queen's favourite outfits, but in fact calling a colour pastel is just another way of saying soft and delicate. A pastel is simply a pale form of a more vibrant shade. As such, it exists in thousands of different tones, and there is one to suit every taste.

When we think of pastels, we often picture a palette inspired by the traditional confectionery shop, complete with Parma violet, marshmallow and bonbon colours. Yet these sweetie shades can evolve when teamed with other colours, taking on a new, more

LOTS OF LOVE
LOTS OF LOVE
LOTS OF LOVE
VINTAGE FABRIC

mature feel. Pastel pink becomes grown up and sensual alongside champagne or ivory, while peach looks serious and subtle next to greys. The intensity and depth of the shade also dictates the impression it creates, so explore the spectrum. A sugared-almond blue may be closely related to a more complex, grey-tinted tone, calling to mind sea and sky, which exists just a few steps along the colour chart. Pastel pink, meanwhile, can be baby-bootie cute, as subtle as an old rose or, when tipping towards salmon, distinctly vintage in feel.

The practical benefits of using pastels are frequently overlooked, which is a shame, because these tones are wonderfully good at creating a cosy atmosphere. Hints of apricot or pink will add warmth to a dark space with predominantly grey light – ideal for north-facing rooms. Pale pastel tones can help a smaller room seem bigger, too. Remember, though, that any shade intensifies

RIGHT *Pastels often make their biggest impact when used in simple, minimal ways. Here, a single pink rose and a small, pale green vase make a perfect pair.*

OPPOSITE *This sofa shows how pastel fabrics can be combined for eye-catching results. Pinks, yellows and lilacs create a candy-coloured kaleidoscope, and, in addition to florals, there are hand-embroidered cushion covers, ginghams, spots and stripes.*

LEFT *This living room takes a more-is-more approach to using pastels. The sofa is layered with a patchwork quilt and a good selection of cushions, but there are also handmade curtains at the window and a rug with ice-cream-coloured stripes.*

RIGHT *Pink wallpaper is used on one wall, with white as the dominant theme in the rest of the room. For cohesion, the pink is picked up in the light, the chair seats and the stationery.*

when painted on all four walls because the colour bounces off itself. So use tester pots and observe how natural and artificial lights affect the shade before you give your room the wall-to-wall treatment.

A block of pastel colour can look surprisingly intense and is not to everyone's taste, but there are ways to introduce pastel tones into a room without painting every wall peach. Use your chosen pastel as an accent. Paint a door or window frame that colour – a great way to frame a view – or simply add a glinting glass door knob or painted chair to a white room.

Pattern can be invaluable in these circumstances. Depending on its design, it can do much to knock the sugary edges off the pastel palette. Don't layer too many different patterns together, though – this can tax the eye – and exercise restraint over how much you use. You might like to hang patterned wallpaper, but a single panel may be enough. Use it to pick out a chimney breast or brighten an alcove, then keep the remaining walls plain. When it comes to the design, favour rambling florals for a vintage vibe or, for a modern take, find a geometric pattern that brings masculine energy to a room. To create a witty clash of colour and design, choose geometrics that incorporate pastel tones.

Patterned fabrics are another almost limitless source of pastel colours and pretty designs, from polka dots and candy stripes to faded florals. Unlike wallpaper, they have the advantage of being easy to move or modify. Scattering a few cushions across your sofa is simple and inexpensive. Similarly, try putting a patterned shade on a plain lamp, throwing a stripy cloth over a table or hanging curtains with a cottage-style motif of spring blooms. Finally, accessorize! Patterned china is abundantly available in pastel colours, whether you are after vintage teacups or contemporary rustic mugs. Check out the melamine homeware by the Danish company Rice, available in a mouthwatering spectrum of delicious shades.

ABOVE LEFT *An antique metal fingerplate adds wonderful detail to a living-room door. Its colours and floral design harmonize well with those on the wallpaper behind.*

LEFT *Pastel paint and wallpaper give character to the walls in this room, but the eye is drawn to the vintage cupboard, with its wooden mouldings picked out in pink. Such decoration represents a pleasing compromise between painting furniture white and painting it entirely in a single pastel colour.*

ABOVE *Often decorated with floral designs in gorgeous colours, vintage china offers an opportunity to enhance your table display with pastel chic. Pick up individual pieces at fairs and markets to create a mismatched collection that can constantly evolve.*

ABOVE RIGHT *If you are wary of using pastels across all four walls, painting details is a fail-safe alternative. Here, the door frame has been painted yellow, while the door wears aqua with touches of turquoise. The effect is quirky but understated.*

RIGHT *Wallpaper is used to zone the space by the front door where shoes are taken off and bags hung up. The pink-painted shelf accentuates the pink notes in the paper, for a casually coordinated feel.*

Furniture and Lighting

Furniture and lighting are the basic ingredients of any room – the objects that help us to work, cook, store our possessions and relax in comfort. But while they are primarily designed for practical purposes, these items can look pastel-pretty, too. Sometimes it takes no more than a simple coat of paint.

Painted walls, patterned cushions, rugs and artwork are often the primary sources of colour in a room, while solid pieces of furniture remain neutral. Pretty-pastel style turns this convention on its head, putting furniture dressed in pastel shades at the front of the stage. A white background will best show off a pink cupboard or a powder-blue chair, but there are no rules. Combine painted furniture with painted walls for an ice-cream effect, or find your favourite tone in a wall of patterned paper and replicate it on a chair or a shelf.

Painting wooden furniture is an excellent way to give large-scale pieces a pastel personality. Old items with wonderful bones but a tired exterior are ripe for a makeover. Sand and prime them, then finish with a top coat in a shade you love. Experiment with a simple shelf first, then work up to tables, armoires, chests of drawers – whatever takes your fancy!

The advantages of painting old furniture are multiple. This is an inexpensive and eco-friendly means of furnishing your home, plus it allows you to choose the colours yourself. If you love the character of old furniture but don't have time to reinvent a piece, there are many independent shops selling restored vintage armoires, cabinets and chairs, but the recent vogue for grey means it can be hard to find pastel-painted examples. Doing it yourself is often the best option.

LEFT *Vintage lighting was often crafted from spray-painted metal. Find original pieces on eBay or buy new. Many home-furnishing stores carry some vintage-inspired lamps and pendant lights in soft colours.*

ABOVE RIGHT *This handsome old cupboard looks festive rather than serious with its coat of pink paint. The colour matches some of the china inside and is extremely soft, creating a subtle but stylish effect.*

RIGHT *The pale painted finish on this grand wooden bed frame helps it to disappear into the white wall behind and look less austere. Instead, the door, painted in pastel green, becomes the focal point.*

Creating a balance of colour – not too much, not too little – is as important when you furnish a room as when you are painting it. So, to avoid pastel fatigue setting in, consider painting some of your second-hand finds white and accessorizing with pastels. It may also be that you don't want, or need, to paint your furniture, but you can still give it pastel appeal. A coloured seat pad will cheer up an old dining chair or soften a design classic.

Look out for new furniture with a pastel finish, too. Even design classics occasionally appear dressed in a colourful new outfit. To celebrate the 60th birthday of Hans Wegner's famous Wishbone Chair, for example, Carl Hansen & Son recently manufactured it in a range of special-edition shades, including citrus grey, light blue and sea green.

It could be the material that dictates a piece's colour – or absence of colour. Furniture manufacturers rarely obscure a beautiful hardwood with a layer of paint, but some metals and plastics lend themselves to colour. The process of powder-coating allows a rainbow of shades to be applied to metal. Consider, for example, Harry Bertoia's Side Chair, available with the trademark steel-lattice construction powder-coated in lush colours.

Coloured plastic and similar synthetic materials are much used for furniture, too, and are often available in pastel tones. Choose from inexpensive moulded-plastic stools and simple stacking chairs with coloured polypropylene shells, or splash out on a design classic like Verner Panton's 'S' Chair in pink or pale blue.

ABOVE *Moderation is key when using strong, sugary pastels. This shade of pink is particularly sweet and dense, and might be hard to live with if used in abundance, so confining it to a chair is a safer way to enjoy it. In this case, the wallpaper's white ground has a cooling effect.*

RIGHT *Pastels are associated with the artificial colours in cakes and candy, but they also occur naturally. Think raw plaster, fresh flowers and even distressed wood. This gorgeous detail belongs to a handsome bed. The off-white paint on this carving has been rubbed down to reveal a pink layer below.*

Wooden furniture looks wonderful painted in pastels. Finding a sensible chest of drawers, such as this one, painted cupcake pink is likely to evoke surprise and pleasure. The white wall behind not only helps it to stand out but also means that this strong shade does not have to fight with other colours.

A vintage table lamp combines beauty with utility. Its movable head makes it a useful task light, while its primrose colour enlivens a white scheme. The hydrangea, popped into an old milk jug, is a similar shade to the lamp, showing that pastel colours are anything but artificial.

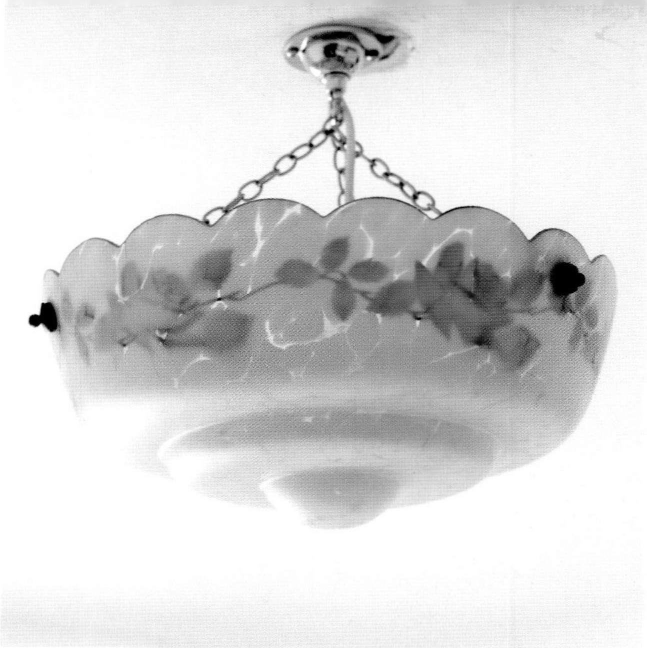

ABOVE *This vintage ceiling light is made from pastel-blue glass with a generous beadwork trim. A characterful piece like this brings depth to any scheme and creates a pocket of detail in the often neglected upper part of a room.*

RIGHT *Decorative lampshades, dripping with trimmings and tassels, were big design news in the 1930s and 1940s, but can look fussy today. That said, they can still find a place in the pretty pastel home. This oversized shade has been used in an all-white dining space, adding a pop of peachy colour and striking a confident retro note.*

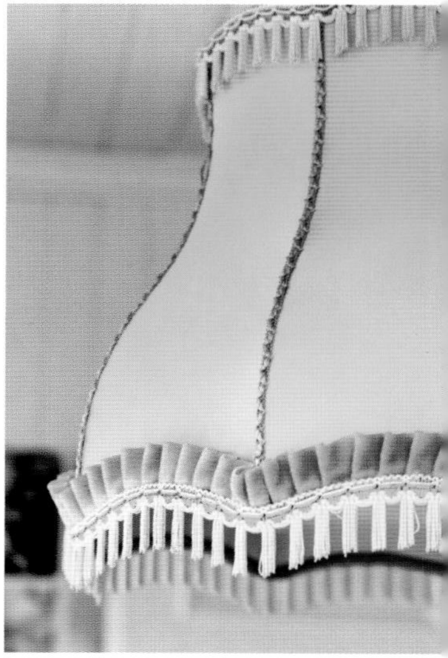

TOP *This 1930s glass ceiling light has a pattern of pink roses around it. Try eBay or your local flea market for something similar. Lighting from this period is not as sought after as industrial vintage pieces and is often relatively inexpensive.*

ABOVE *Although lighting must perform a range of functions and tasks, allowing us to have a life after dark, it can be playful and decorative, too. This wall light, shaped as a question mark, looks like a piece of illuminated art.*

Lighting performs a serious role, helping us to carry on with ordinary activities after dark. It is still possible to have some pastel fun with it, though! Hunt around on eBay, as vintage lighting often comes in pastel colours. You might find a metal ceiling pendant in pale blue or minty green, or a classic Anglepoise lamp; these lamps were typically sprayed white or black, but sometimes crop up in softer shades, from rose to avocado. When it comes to table or wall lights, finish them with pastel lampshades, but remember that, once the bulb inside is illuminated, the colour will appear lighter. Alternatively, add a twist of colour by fitting ceiling pendants with old-style textile cable, available in various shades.

TUINBLOEMEN
The Allotment Book
IN THE CITY
Paris Interiors
New York Interiors
British Style
BELLE BLANC
thuis
HOME
DECORATING
pattern
Decorate
beautiful leaves of canada

LEFT *Books, magazines and stationery are stacked so neatly on this white shelving unit that they look highly decorative. Their colours add personality to the space and draw the eye to them, but, rather than leave the shelves as the room's sole focal point, wallpaper, lighting and seating in pink have been used to round out the scheme.*

RIGHT *The bed and chest of drawers in this elegant bedroom are painted an off-white colour. The bed is a large piece in quite a small room, and this soft shade helps it to blend in. A vintage ceiling light and old-fashioned eiderdown introduce welcome pattern, enlivening the knocked-back colour scheme.*

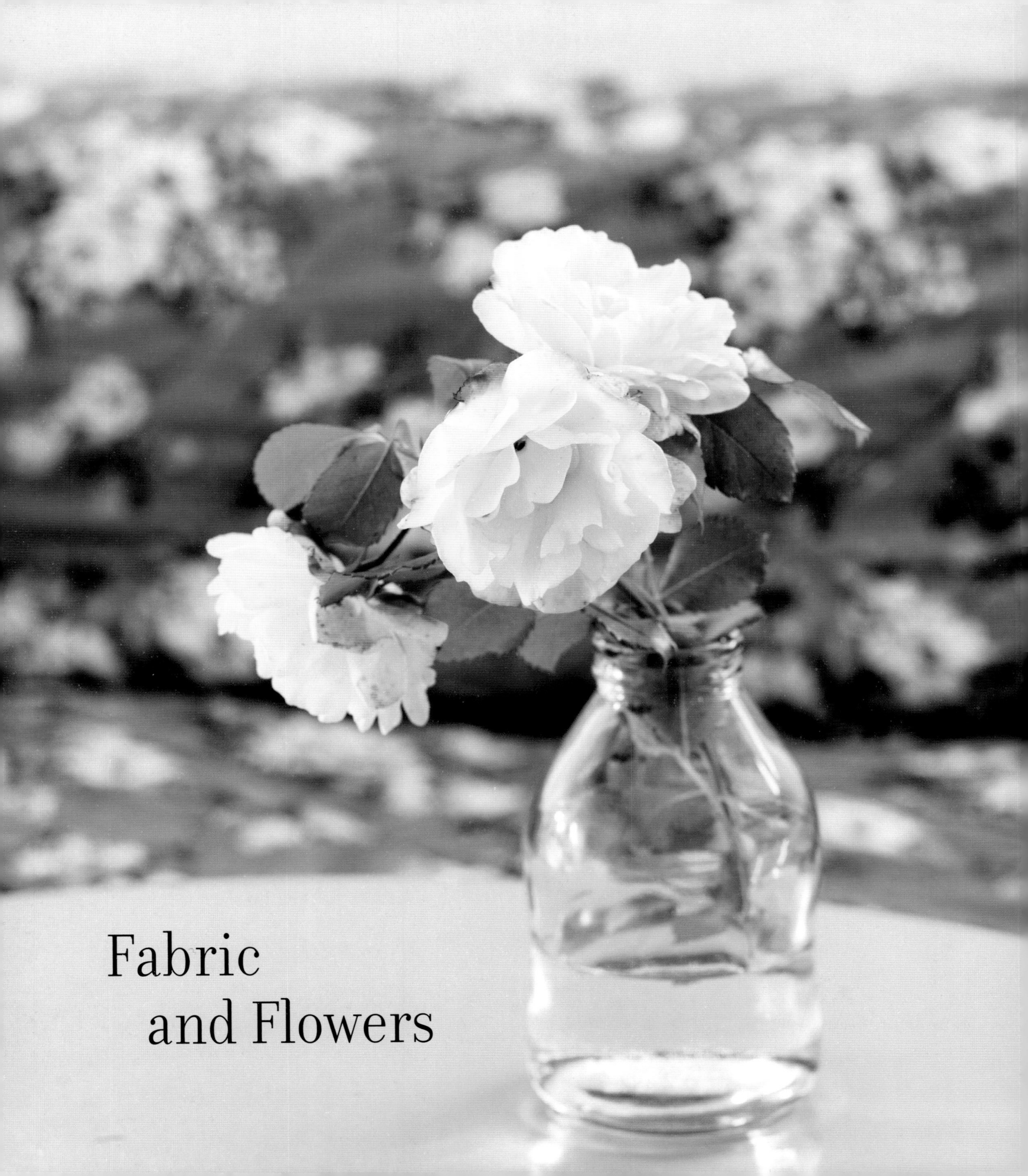

Fabric and Flowers

Whether you choose cheerful gingham, faded chintz or a retro repeat in candy colours, patterned fabrics look beautiful in any pastel room. Incorporate them in cushion covers, bed linen, tablecloths and more, then mirror their pretty tones with bunches of freshly cut flowers, casually arranged in vases and jars.

From the blossom on a plum tree to the fragrant roses of summer, flowers come in numerous colours and shapes that delight and seduce us. So whether you have a garden full of flourishing plants or buy cut flowers from a local florist, bring some natural beauty into your home. Fresh blooms are a marvellous addition to any room, filling it with organic colour and delicate fragrance. Best of all, they come in a rainbow of pretty pastel shades.

When shopping for flowers, choose gentle hues. Roses offer a great choice of pastels, from faded peach to milky pink, but don't be restricted by flower variety. Mix different blooms to create a relaxed posy or simply display a single stem. If your cupboards are not crammed with vases, don't worry – anything from a pitcher to a jam jar will make the ideal home.

ABOVE *Beautiful clothing deserves to be put on display. In this bedroom, a summery blouse, hung from a curtain rail, adds floral pattern and pastel colour to the scheme.*

LEFT *Many flowers come in delicate colours, so you are spoilt for choice when picking a pastel bunch. Roses, particularly classic old varieties, are often pastel toned and provide natural inspiration for a room's colour scheme.*

RIGHT *Lace curtains and a blind made from white fabric with a design of hand-drawn birds create an understated backdrop to this old wooden windowsill, which has been brightened up by a row of pastel pots and vivid blooms.*

Cherry blossom signals the arrival of spring and is celebrated around the world for its beauty. It comes in lovely pastel colours, from soft pink to delicate coral.

Think about where you place your flowers. They may make a wonderful centrepiece on a table laid with vintage china, but try them in more surprising locations, too. Find space for a bunch of cottage blooms in your hallway so that they are the first thing you see on returning home, or start your day with an inspiring vision by popping flowers into a vase on your bedside table. Remember to use cut flowers in outdoor as well as indoor spaces. A dark, enclosed courtyard or grassy garden will particularly benefit from a bunch on a patio table.

For as long as we have been enjoying flowers in our homes, we have also been stitching, printing and weaving them onto fabric. These artificial blooms come in every size and style, so it is easy to find a print that works with your pretty pastel room. Roses are a favourite motif, but a little shopping around will reveal textiles adorned with a huge range of blooms – everything from poppies to water lilies.

ABOVE *Paper cups may be disposable party essentials, but that doesn't mean they have to be plain. These cups and drinking straws add a decorative touch to the festive table.*

This home, made predominantly from wood, stands on the beach and its aqua scheme reflects its location. To invigorate the blue, the table is dressed with pink-striped fabric, topped with a smaller vintage tablecloth in a floral design.

Ramp up the colour content by choosing fabric entirely in pastel colours, or create a cottage-style vibe with a small-scale design against a neutral background. Balance these decorative textiles with plain pastel fabrics, or look out for ginghams, spots and stripes. You can work floral fabrics into your rooms on items such as napkins or cushion covers, or be bold and use them for upholstery, curtains and blinds. For a finishing touch, plunder your clothes closet. Hang a delicate floral blouse from a closet door or drape a vintage scarf over a lampshade for another splash of pretty pastel pattern.

LEFT *This beautifully laid table is a shrine to fabrics and flowers. Place mats embroidered with posies and china decorated with flowers in airy pastel shades, and plenty of romantic roses dotted here and there, create an irresistible teatime spot.*

ABOVE *Large bunches of flowers are always impressive, but there is much to enjoy when just a few blooms are displayed casually like this. You can really appreciate each flower and even a modest jam jar makes a fitting container.*

ABOVE *Patchwork drawstring bags stitched from old floral sheets and tablecloths make pretty storage on this peg rail and are fun and inexpensive to produce. Roses popped into jars and glasses on the shelf above add further pastel notes and are a great contrast to the green wall behind.*

Display and Decoration

A plate rack is a flexible, decorative addition to a wall, while framing old wallpaper makes a great artwork. Here, in another amusing touch, a ceramic stag's head has been added.

No pretty pastel room is complete without a smattering of softly coloured objects. Whether you are displaying ceramics or sketches, books or beads, keep the dial set to pastel for a pretty, relaxed feel and think creatively, too – even the most unlikely objects, when arranged imaginatively, can look fantastic.

With your furniture and backdrop in place, you are ready to style your home. This is the time when you can let your imagination run free and enjoy grouping, hanging, framing and displaying your treasured possessions and quirky finds. Even if your rooms are neutral at this stage, you can still nudge them towards a pretty pastel look, using decorative pieces in a rainbow of soft shades.

OPPOSITE *A table set with pastel treats on pretty plates and cups awaits the party guests. Coloured papers folded into fan shapes add further decoration, while paper globes and lengths of ribbon tied to a string form the colourful backdrop.*

ABOVE *Finding new roles for familiar pieces can make it easier to create arresting and unusual displays. Here, a china teacup and saucer have been reinvented as a candle, making a lovely addition to a mantelpiece among a host of other coloured ceramics.*

RIGHT *This close-up shot of a shelving unit reveals how even practical items can look beautiful when thoughtfully arranged. A pink theme runs through this display, but there are no rules about what can make it onto the shelf. Bright nail varnish, ribbon, hair clips and jewellery look decorative when allowed space to breathe. They are teamed with an eclectic mixture of china, books and other objects, which introduces flashes of gold, orange and purple to the scene.*

Pictures, china and books are invaluable decorative ingredients of any room, but almost any object can make a visual impact when displayed thoughtfully. In fact, it's often the more unusual items that make the most eye-catching features, and when they come dressed in soft, appealing tones, they brilliantly boost the pastel content of the room, too.

A handful of cotton reels strung on a wire; folded napkins, stacked up in a pile; beads draped from a mirror or bedhead; pretty postcards taped to a wall – all these items could be stored in drawers or boxes, but arranging them creatively allows their colour and form to be enjoyed every day and creates pockets of interest.

The display possibilities of everyday items are often overlooked, and yet so many practical pieces are pretty, too. China is an obvious example. Display your favourite pastel plates and cups on open shelves, racks or hooks so that you can admire their varied colours when not in use. Stationery items or pencils are beautifully colourful and look great when neatly arranged in trays or pots. Craft essentials such as wool, buttons and ribbon can also bring welcome pastel colour to a room, while in the bathroom, pretty soaps and colourful nail polishes continue the pastel theme. As long as you consciously arrange these pieces, they will serve a decorative as well as a practical purpose.

Nous deux
WETLOOK
VINTAGE RIBBON
AUSTR
Jacques
Spiegel

When hung in a carefully chosen spot, this beautiful slip becomes a work of art rather than a piece of clothing. Light from the window floods through the delicate fabric, lightening its pink colour and showing off the lacework detail. A blind made from a length of vintage lace makes a fittingly romantic backdrop.

The quickest way to give a room a new feel is to move your collections around, so whatever you display, whether it's a set of pastel coffee cups or a still-life painting, keep flexibility in mind. Consider propping pictures against a wall rather than hanging them, or simply tack up postcards or cuttings with tape. An original idea for displaying unframed prints or photos is to hang them from a pin using a bulldog clip. Similarly, instead of hanging plates, stand them on shelves so that you can easily play around with the arrangement – and use them, too! Then, every once in a while, dismantle your displays and have fun regrouping your treasured pieces, for a fresh, fast makeover.

ABOVE *A simple, functional blackboard takes on a decorative feel thanks to its pink frame. This candy colour makes a strong and unusual contrast to the black writing surface, but ties in beautifully with the pink on the spotted curtains hanging next to it.*

ABOVE RIGHT *Displaying colourful plates and platters on open shelving like this is the easiest way to show them off. Ideally, install shelves with a small lip at the front, to prevent the plates from slipping.*

ABOVE RIGHT *A humble hook in the wall can be the starting point for a colourful, funky display. Here, beads and sunglasses bring shots of fun and colour to a wall covered in demure floral paper.*

RIGHT *High shelves are home to a selection of framed images, china and personal treasures. A further 'break-out' display of pictures taped informally to the wall sits below, making a pleasing foil to the neatly arranged collection above.*

Mix and Match

We all know that variety is the spice of life – and it's a key component of pretty pastel style, too. So pep up those fancy fondant shades with a rich mixture of materials, textures and finishes. Witty contrasts, surprising combinations and layers of interest will keep these gentle colours fresh and fun.

OPPOSITE *A huge variety of fabrics, from vintage offcuts to ginghams, has been used in this vibrant living space – and it is the layering of so many patterns that creates the winningly quirky feel.*

ABOVE *White walls and black shiny worktops are cleverly stripped of all their austere, sleek feel by the addition of china and glassware in a rainbow of powdery pastels.*

Pretty pastel style has a huge colour palette of soft tones as its foundation, but these can be incorporated into your home in anything from textiles, paint and wallpaper to furniture, artwork and ceramics. A combination of all these ingredients works best, so try mixing materials, patterns and finishes to create maximum impact, while also giving some texture and weight to this airy, feminine palette.

By mixing pastels with contrasting tones, you can make sure that the style remains colourful without becoming sugary. Offset the sweetness of pastels by teaming them with plenty of white, which allows the soft colour to shine out, but prevents it overpowering a room. Alternatively, be brave and balance these pale shades with black. It may seem an unlikely

This room breaks all the design rules, mixing soft pastel green with saturated egg-yolk yellow, then sticking a vast, black piano in the middle. With plenty of white on the ceiling, floor and one wall, the disparate pieces work together, looking striking and brave rather than chaotic.

pairing but, used in moderation, black does much to anchor pastel colours, at the same time as providing a dramatic backdrop that really accentuates these subtle tones. It is a surprising mixture, which brings edgy cool to a pretty pastel scheme.

Be sure to mix up materials and finishes, too. Eggshell paint creates a soft, chalky finish on woodwork, but experiment with gloss, too, for a more dramatic, light-reflecting surface. Use it sparingly, on a door frame or simple shelf, for a pop of pastel with a touch of shine. In a cooking space, display elegant vintage china alongside contemporary pastel-coloured plastics or retro enamelware, to keep the colour scheme exciting and original. Underfoot, soften smart white floorboards with a pastel rag rug or fluffy, dyed sheepskin. On a sofa, scatter cushions in a range of textiles and textures.

ABOVE *When a dessert is as bright as this cheesecake, it looks best served on plain china with a pale finish.*

RIGHT *Layers of upbeat pastels – on the wallpaper, paintwork and shopping bags – create a colourful display in a hallway.*

LEFT *Sriking jewellery in a riot of vibrant colours looks attractive thrown onto a vintage plate. Displaying it this way also makes it easy to select pieces to wear.*

Mixing and matching has practical benefits, too. A dinner service put together from random pieces of pastel china, picked up at junk shops and fairs, looks beautiful and is easy to add to. If you break a piece, you can enjoy rummaging around at your next yard or garage sale for an inexpensive replacement. So long as it shares the same pastel colour scheme, it will fit in.

Similarly, stitching together a mix of small fabric swatches to make a patchwork throw or curtains is an excellent way to employ these otherwise useless scraps. The result is a wonderful clash of patterns and pastel shades, which energizes these familiar pinks, lilacs and mints and turns them into something far more interesting. It's all about unexpected combinations and brave contrasts – anything that keeps the pastel palette looking innovative, original and charming.

RIGHT *Keep pastels the cool side of sweet by combining them with plenty of white – or try the opposite approach and mix them with stronger versions of themselves. Here, pale china is displayed in a cupboard, but it is the three bright trays that catch the eye. Painting a yellow backdrop on this section of wall enhances the bold, layered effect, while flowers remind us that this is a colour scheme inspired by the cottage garden as much as by the candy store.*

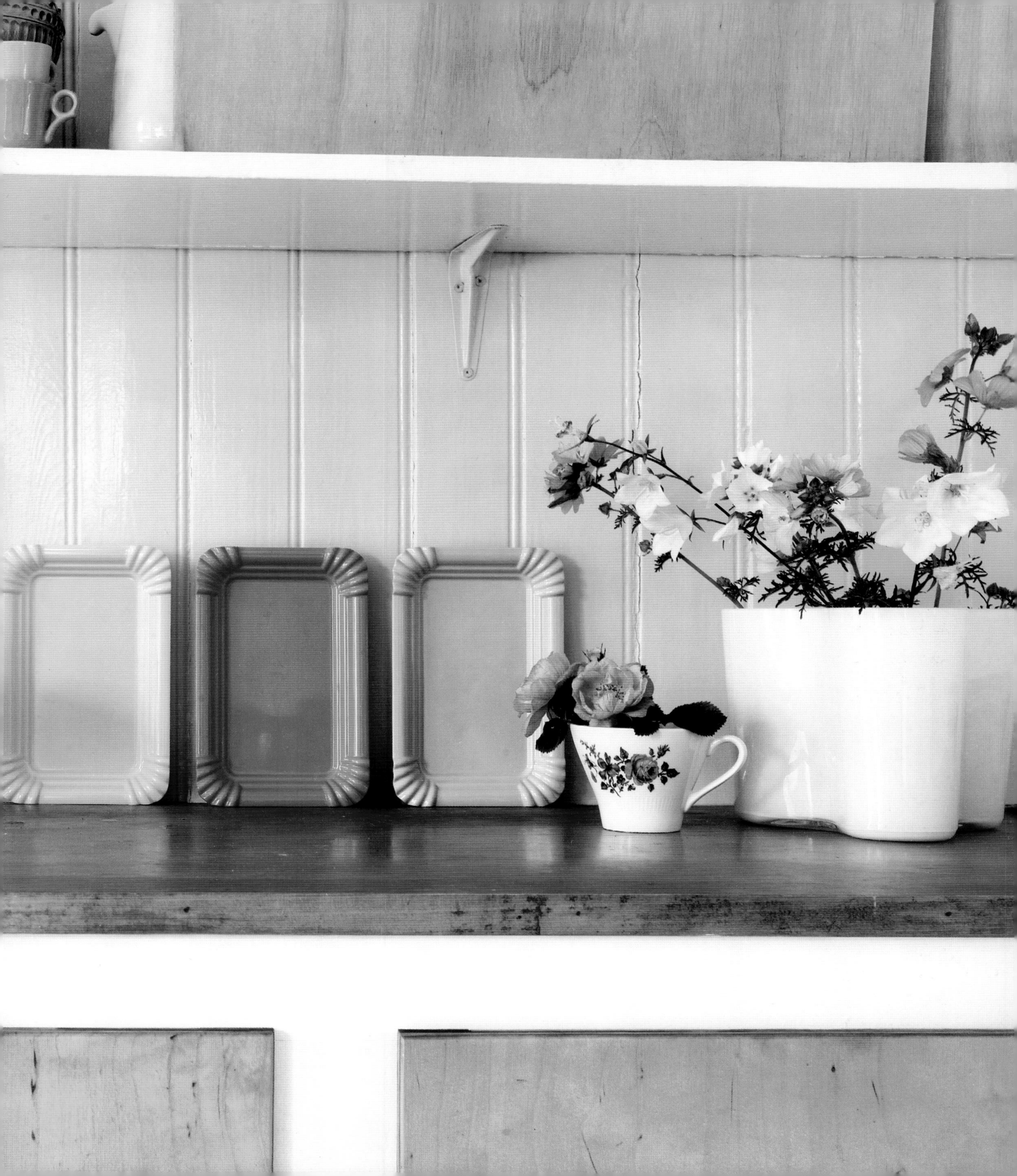

Spaces

Cooking and Eating

A pretty pastel cooking and eating space is a harmonious marriage between form and function, combining practicality with pleasing colour. Use this easy, breezy palette to soften a chic modern kitchen, or create a more homespun effect with a rainbow of soft tones, on everything from the cooker to the cupboards.

Most homes today have a combined cooking and eating space. This may be a large, open-plan area with a big dining table as its focus, perfect for family gatherings. Or it could be a simple galley kitchen with a flip-up table or slim built-in bench. Both styles illustrate the same point: we want to eat where we cook, for both practical and emotional reasons.

Obviously, it is easier to set a table and bring food to it when the cooker, cupboards and refrigerator are all within close proximity. Beyond practicalities, though, there is something uniquely appealing about a busy kitchen. Here, children can play, teenagers can

LEFT *A ceramic dish is used to store a colourful mixture of cooking ingredients and utensils, from measuring spoons to cake flavourings. Tins in pastel colours make useful small-scale storage, while a jug is the perfect home for pastry brushes.*

RIGHT *Cream walls, white units and wooden worktops can be transformed from neutral to colourful with a few pastel touches. Better still, here, the colour is more than simply decorative. It is found on essentials such as dishcloths and pans.*

7 6 5
boter
kaas
ei
JAMIE OLIVER
Rachel Allen
NIGELLA EXPRESS
surinaams kookboek
jam it, pickle it, cure it
July
August
September
October
November
December
Cath Kidston
RIVER COTTAGE YEAR

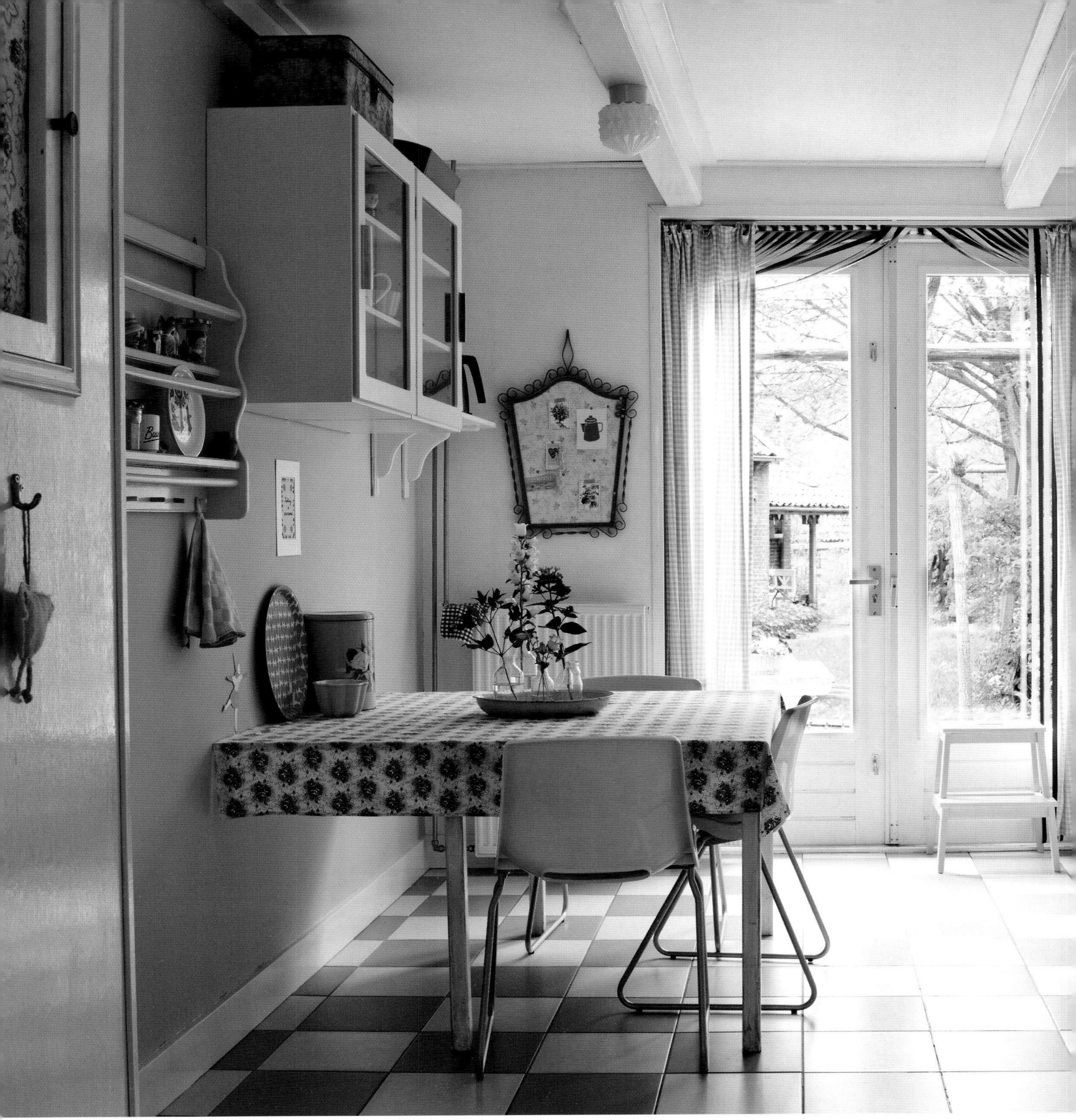

do homework and adults can cook or entertain – all in the same place at the same time. Which other room works as hard? Its multi-tasking personality is central to the success of a cooking and eating space, but designed with pretty pastel style it becomes a joyful, colourful hub as well.

Cooking spaces can be rather serious. When designing from scratch, the initial considerations are practical. Where should the dishwasher be sited in relation to the sink? Is a freestanding oven preferable to a built-in model? How stain resistant is that work surface? How easy to clean is that splashback?

Get the answers to these questions right and your cooking space will function smoothly and efficiently, making the daily rituals of food preparation a pleasure rather than a chore. But, while considering the practical issues, give a thought to aesthetics. Sometimes, it's not how smoothly your cabinet drawers close that matters most; it's how the overall space makes you feel.

A cheerful, soothing pastel palette can be worked into a cooking and eating space in all sorts of ways. Painting walls a pastel shade will warm up a cool space and, since a pastel scheme is usually associated with private rooms, such as bedrooms, it can bring a refreshing, surprising dose of frivolity to a public part of the house. But don't rule out the idea of using a neutral colour on the walls of your cooking and eating space. There are so many other opportunities to bring pastel tones into this room, from china to tea towels, that you may prefer to let the details do the work.

LEFT *The owner of this kitchen has used pastels throughout. Colourful chairs, painted storage, pale blue curtains and pale grey tiles in the chequerboard floor add subtle colour. White units and abundant natural light keep the look fresh.*

RIGHT *China is readily available in pastel colours. These espresso cups in sugared-almond shades make a gorgeous display. Too pretty to be stored behind closed cupboard doors, they look appealing stacked in pairs.*

The same goes for flooring. Choose something fairly neutral that won't fight for attention in a busy scheme. Wooden flooring, stone, poured concrete or ceramic tiles are all tough and easy to clean. Use colour sparingly. Try a chequerboard pattern of white and pastel tiles, paint boards a creamy tone, or simply lay rugs. If you do choose rugs, make sure that they are washable and hard-wearing – this room sees plenty of traffic and spills – then use them to zone the different areas in a large, open-plan space.

A neutral wooden countertop makes a warm, simple backdrop to pastel cookware or units – or be bold and opt for a composite or moulded synthetic material such as Corian, available in numerous colours. Tiles are a classic splashback choice and come in every shade. Use just one colour for a block of pastel or a handful for a patchwork effect.

Whether you are designing a kitchen from scratch or restyling your existing space, consider using a mix of built-in and freestanding cupboards for a relaxed, characterful look. Old armoires can be converted into larder-style storage, while wall cabinets and shelving units are easy to find at second-hand stores. Paint them a soft pastel shade to pull in more colour, or leave the wood untreated and paint the interior, for a flash of pastel when you open a door.

If your existing units are wooden but are crying out for a pastel makeover, sand them down and repaint them. If they have seen better days, take the

ABOVE *Pastels have been freely mixed together in this pretty kitchen but, since the tones come from the same colour family, the effect is harmonious and attractive.*

LEFT *Cheerful pink looks at home in this relaxed kitchen, which combines built-in and freestanding furniture. Practical pieces such as the radio and china and decorative items like the flowers pick up the theme.*

RIGHT *The wall behind this cooking hob has been papered with a design by Piet Hein Eek that resembles planks of coloured wood. An old window protects it from splashes.*

Pretty ceramic cups, bowls and tins, carefully displayed in neat rows and stacks, brighten up these open shelves. Traditional Scandinavian storage, consisting of a row of pale blue drawers for holding cooking ingredients, has been installed beneath it.

doors off and, for an informal, cottage-style look, hang patterned curtains in front of the interior shelves instead. Remember to ignore convention, too. Who says all your units should be the same colour? Paint drawers a pastel tone alongside cabinet doors in white or cool cream.

Another imaginative way to introduce pretty pastel style to your kitchen is through appliances. Often termed white goods because they are traditionally made in that colour, virtually all appliances, from coffee makers to food processors, are available in perky pastel shades. You might also want to invest in a large, iconic piece, such as a 1950s-style refrigerator in an ice-cream tone – Smeg's FAB range is a good place to start – or a built-in oven in a candy colour. Some pieces can even be made to a shade of your specification. Britannia, for example, offers a colour-matching service on a selection of its range cookers.

Since a kitchen often doubles as a space to relax, chat, read, work or socialize, other furniture will be placed alongside your

ABOVE *All kinds of electrical gadgets come in pastel colours. This coffee machine looks fun in pink, but you can source anything, from refrigerators and cookers to measuring scales and food processors, in soft tones for a satisfying marriage of form and function.*

LEFT *Graphic stripes in bold pink, like those seen on the paper bags in traditional candy stores, make a strong contrast with the delicate flowers on these glasses. A good way to keep a pastel scheme looking vibrant is to incorporate clashing patterns.*

ABOVE *This cooking and eating space forms part of an open-plan ground floor. Colours from the same pastel palette are used throughout, with the pinks and purples on the sofa's throw and cushions also found in items of storage, china and glassware.*

OPPOSITE, BELOW LEFT *It is the dainty shape as well as the delicate colour and design that make this china so appealing. Drinking tea from such fine china can transform the simple enjoyment of an everyday cuppa into a special experience.*

functional kitchen cabinets. Choose a pastel-painted wooden table and chairs or put a squashy pink armchair in a comfortable corner. Have fun taking your colour inspiration from the teatime treats you may serve here: fruity yogurts, crisp macaroons, sorbets, iced gems and jam tarts.

There is no need to change your existing kitchen fittings to create a pretty pastel look. Just a few pastel touches, dotted here and there, can give a multi-tasking cooking and eating space real personality. A shelf dotted with teacups in soft shades can soften the austerity of sleek modern units without obstructing the ergonomic feel, while a cloth with pastel spots or a selection of mismatched vintage napkins will make the table an attractive focal point.

If pretty accessories are not your style, don't worry. Bringing pastel touches to a cooking space is about more than styling; these colours are found in many practical objects. Look out for cookware in soft tones, for example. Cast-iron pans and casseroles, such as those made by the French firm Le Creuset, traditionally came in bright volcanic orange, but they are now available enamelled in a huge range of colours, from soft almond to rose.

Other cookware, whether newly made or second hand, comes dressed in pastel notes. Colanders, scales, measuring spoons, timers and even just the handle on a serving spoon can be pink rather than plain. For a warm, informal feel, put your equipment and utensils on display so that you can enjoy their shapes and colours when not in use. Hang them from butcher's hooks on a simple metal rail, or pile them into jars, pitchers or canisters.

Tableware is a more obvious vehicle for spreading pastel hues across your cooking and eating space. China in strong candy-coloured shades conveys a

ABOVE *Rather than a completely matching set, this cup, milk jug and teapot share the same design and shape but come in different pastel tones, for visual variety. The spotted plate adds more pastel colour to this service.*

RIGHT *Teatime treats such as fondant fancies and macaroons come in gorgeous pastel shades, but so do many favourites from the dessert trolley. Served on vintage china, fresh melon and a pink raspberry cheesecake look as good as they taste.*

LEFT *Decorative packaging can be enjoyed in any pretty pastel space. These beautiful boxes of fruit pastilles are covered in gorgeous wrappers and make a decorative stack brimming with colour and pattern.*

BELOW LEFT *Painted wooden furniture gives this roomy eating space a relaxed feel. The large table in duck-egg blue is flanked by chairs in pale blue-grey, salmon pink and white. Hot pink on the wall frames the scene beautifully.*

BELOW *Forget boring plain white sugar lumps. This sugar has been coloured and shaped to look wonderfully decorative – and it's the perfect way to add pastel tones to your morning cup of coffee.*

RIGHT *Vintage tins and chintzy fabric give this sink area a cottage-like feel. Practical items such as this fluffy duster are often made in vibrant colours.*

modern feel, especially when teamed with pieces in saturated brights, while pretty polka-dot pottery introduces a cottage-style feel.

You can have fun mixing up pastels in every hue and material, from modern melamine to fine bone china and chunky earthenware. Display your prize pieces on open shelves for an eclectic look, or simply introduce a show-stopper vase or cake stand into a simple white scheme for a pure pop of pastel.

Compared to a living room or bedroom, many of the surfaces in a cooking space are hard and unadorned, designed primarily with practicality in mind – countertops, shiny hotplates, floors that are resilient and easy to sweep. But you can nevertheless bring some tactile textiles and fabrics into this room, which will contribute welcome warmth. Set the table with a pastel tablecloth or linen placemats, for example. Create seat cushions for dining chairs

or a long bolster for a bench and use patterned throws to brighten up an armchair or sofa.

Next, look at the details. Complete a table with pastel napkins. Tiny retro repeats look jolly – channel that 1950s street-party feel – as do simple paper serviettes with a cute design of clouds or candy stripes. There is no need to stop here, though. Tea towels, ironing board covers, oven gloves and aprons can all be found in pastel-coloured fabrics and pretty patterns. These incidental pieces are fun to shop for, inexpensive to buy and will effortlessly complete your pastel scheme.

ABOVE *In a compact dining area, consider using a circular rather than square or oblong table, which is often better suited to the shape of the space, as well as being more sociable. Wallpaper on the far wall draws the eye, creating an illusion of depth.*

Living and Relaxing

The days when homes contained a formal parlour have long since passed. Today's living spaces are devoted to relaxation. Choose comfortable furniture, introduce favourite treasures – but, most importantly, work in colour from the pastel palette. Dusky or cheeky, muted or bold, these versatile tones will add personality to a much-loved space.

A combined cooking and eating space is often our most frequently used room, but the living room is still a cherished part of any home. Its primary role is as a haven for relaxation. Here, you can curl up in a cosy armchair with a book or stretch out on a sofa to watch a movie. With space at a premium in so many modern homes, the living room may be required to perform various other tasks, depending on the time of day or even the time of year. So, before reaching for your paintbrush, think first about how you use this valuable public room.

RIGHT *This elegant living space has the feel of a French chateau, even though the house is in England. The furniture is curvy, while details such as the half-panelled walls and double doors carry hints of grandeur. This impression is enhanced by a pastel palette of watery pinks and greens.*

HIP HOTELS FRANCE
HIP HOTELS CITY
HIP HOTELS ESCAPE

Defining the true identity of your living space will bring you closer to choosing the right pastel shades for it. Is it a place for family television sessions on a Saturday night or an adult space for drinks and conversation? Is it a small cosy snug or a large multi-tasking area that doubles as an office or spare room?

Think next about how best to reflect the room's purpose through the colours you use in it. Pastels can look jolly and fun; or subtle and understated. If you are seeking a sophisticated, grown-up feel for your sophisticated, grown-up living room, then pick pastels from the complex, muted end of the spectrum. Think blues and lavenders with plenty of grey in them, faded-apricot or raw-plaster shades, berry tones and even a touch of gold.

If, on the other hand, your living space is a busy family hub, full of life and activity, then brighter tones and lipstick shades will work well in it. It is hard to generalize about pastels, since they are available in such a huge variety, but as a rule of thumb when thinking about the impression a pastel will create, remember that pink is playful, lavenders and blues are calming, greens are spring-like and optimistic, while yellows are fresh and sunny.

ABOVE *Pale pink and leaf green are a perfect pairing, found in wild flowers or blossoming cherry trees. The colours may be natural, but these cushions, with their frilly trim, are a playful touch on a sensible sofa.*

RIGHT *This living space is filled with quirky details, from the gold bunting to the retro lampshade and painted Ercol chairs. It works because the floor, walls and ceiling are white, providing a fresh background for the mixture of disparate pieces.*

OPPOSITE *Muted pastels are used here for a restrained feel. Soft pinks and greens are teamed with stripped boards and retro touches, such as the lamp. Fresh flowers become a focal point, their colours similar to, but more vibrant than, the backdrop.*

fashion illustration by fashion designers
LONDON
TALKING FASHION SARAJANE HOARE

Scrutinizing how you use your living space will also help to highlight any problems with its design. If it is under-used, ask yourself why. Does it lack natural light or suffer from too much sun and glare? Does it feel small or featureless? Once you have pinpointed the problem, you can tackle it using pastels. Blue tones will soothe, cooling down a sun-drenched room and giving it an airy rather than a garish feel, yet pastels with peach or primrose-yellow tones will brighten a dark space. Very pale pastels and off-whites, meanwhile, will reflect as opposed to absorb light, so they will increase the feeling of space in a small room.

Soft pink and green are the predominant colours in this living room, chosen because they soften up a large, grand space and give it a playful, intimate feel.

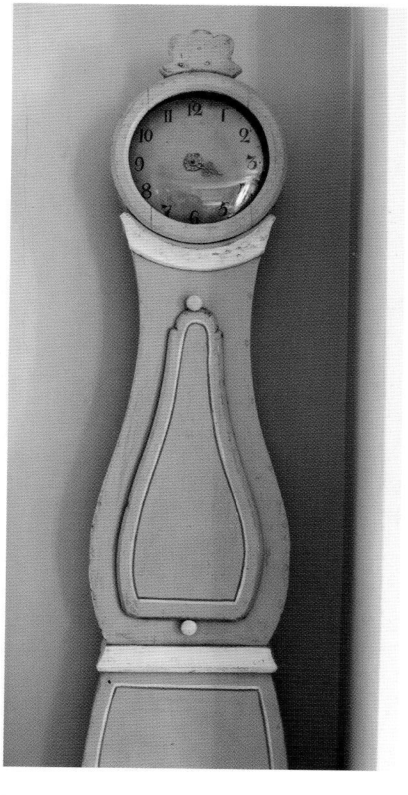

LEFT *Unlike grandfather clocks in the English style, with their dark wooden casing and imposing size, this traditional Swedish design is smaller and curvier. Its clock face is pleasingly modest in size, while the woodwork is painted a soft green.*

OPPOSITE *This room features a daring combination of antique furniture and modern classics, such as the Bubble Chair by Eero Aarnio and the Tulip Table by Eero Saarinen. A colour scheme of pink and green holds the look together.*

When you have discovered the shades that best express your living space and the people who enjoy it, think about where to use them. Walls are the largest surface area in any room and, when painted, will deliver the biggest colour punch. For this reason, use paint carefully on walls. Pretty pastel style is about balancing different tones rather than having one very definite shade. Try painting all four walls in an off-white, then punctuating the expanse with pops of richer pastel. Alternatively, use a lush, chalky colour as an accent on a chimney breast or behind bookshelves. When it comes to using pastels, less is often more.

Think about how pastels interact with other colours and materials, too, and make them work for you. Use them to tone down bolder shades. A collection of bright-green glassware

LEFT *A plain cushion is teamed with a delicate pastel design picked out with tiny touches of bright colour, to bring understated detail to a sofa.*

OPPOSITE *Even a small splash of soft pastel colour can transform the feel of a room. This living space would look rather serious dressed solely in white and grey, but the addition of a pink throw on the sofa introduces softness and personality. A single flower adds a bright accent.*

ABOVE *Simple and elegant, this living space uses pastels with great care and delicacy, preferring the pieces, rather than the colours, to take centre stage. This beautiful old chair has a frame painted in the palest grey, while a single pink flower on the windowsill gently punctuates the white scheme.*

Wooden boards are the stars in this simple attic room. Painting a few on the far wall in pastel blue and cream and teaming them with boards with a distressed finish gives the space life and personality.

could look eye-wateringly stark against a white wall, but, if it's set against a wall painted a pastel version of the same green, the effect is calmer and more cohesive. Pastels are also expert at prettifying rough features such as exposed brickwork and industrial finishes like concrete or stainless steel.

After walls, the floor is the second greatest surface area in your living space. Depending on the purposes for which the room is used, the floor could see a great deal of traffic, or very little. Carpet offers luxury and softness underfoot, but pretty pastel style favours a cleaner, crisper look. So choose a hard surface, such as wooden boards, that will also enhance the atmosphere of the room. White or pale painted floorboards will boost light levels and freshen up candy colours, while old, scuffed boards provide an unpretentious antidote to an extra-sweet pastel scheme.

Any hard flooring can be softened and brightened with rugs. Rugs give you the chance to bring pastel pattern and colour to floor level, but they can also be used to create different zones in a space. Place one under a coffee table close to a sofa, to mark

ABOVE *This seating is built into a sun-filled porch, overlooking the garden. A foam pad covered in striped fabric forms the base, topped with an assortment of cushions in complementary pale tones; a single pink 'rabbit' cushion creates a focal point.*

LEFT *This spectacular ornate sofa was found in India. The green patterned fabric is the original upholstery, but the owner painted the wooden frame a pale green to echo other pastel notes in the room.*

out this area as a cosy, sociable spot. In an open-plan room, use them to show where the area for relaxation begins. Tough, machine-washable flat-woven rugs are perfect for any high-traffic parts of your home. Save deeper pile or antique rugs for quieter corners. Think about size as well. Small rugs are easy to move around, instantly refreshing the feel of a room, whereas large rugs are frequently bought for a specific place and cannot be accommodated anywhere else.

If the basic structure and character of your living space are looking good and you simply want a style makeover, you can easily achieve a pretty pastel look incorporating this palette in soft furnishings and accessories. Before you rush out and buy a new pink armchair, though, consider reupholstering an existing piece. Choose a classic ticking

ABOVE *This living space illustrates how easy it is to introduce pastels into a room by means of small-scale items. Simply keep walls and flooring neutral, add a single painted chair or floral cushion, then layer up the pattern and colour as you wish.*

RIGHT *A dramatic combination of pink and rough brickwork make this balcony, which is several floors above ground level, look pretty and gritty at the same time. Paper decorations and pom-poms soften the look and lead the eye up and down the wall.*

This sofa has been given a patchwork-style covering by simply stretching lengths of patterned and striped fabric over its frame and cushions. It is an easy, inexpensive way to give a large piece of furniture a new look.

stripe in seaside colours for coastal chic, or go for fabric that pairs unusual combinations of pastels and prints for some welcome edge. A classic houndstooth or tartan print, for example, looks fresh and witty in a pastel shade.

Explore the world of pastel plains, too. Thick linens or slubby silks in pastel tones will take the serious edge off a modern modular sofa with strong lines, for example. Teaming pastels with contemporary designs is also a wonderful way to bring the palette up to date. Alternatively, you can achieve a similar effect with slipcovers, which are easy to remove for cleaning, or simply spread a pastel throw or blanket over a neutral sofa or armchair.

Curtains and blinds perform a practical function, providing privacy and insulating the room, but they can also be made to reflect and reinforce the pastel scheme. In a vintage-style room, for example, use a plain silk or muslin and design the curtains to be extra long to create romantic, billowing pools at floor level. In a modern pastel space, stick to plain roller-blinds in a fresh

ABOVE *The pattern of leaves and flowers has been painted by hand onto the walls as a highly distinctive alternative to wallpaper. Old-fashioned radiators and tall wooden window shutters in soft green also contribute to the faded, vintage style.*

RIGHT *A console table painted sage green is dotted with vintage pieces in pastel tones. The mirror is propped up, rather than hung, in order to avoid damaging the wall's unique hand-painted design. The roses match the pinkish wall behind.*

LEFT *Brave colour combinations give this hallway an invigorating look. A gorgeous arrangement of individual pink blooms on the table stands out against a wall covered in a fresh yellow wallpaper.*

OPPOSITE *Pastel tones and plenty of texture enhance the comfort of this living room. The vintage sofa is upholstered in candy stripes, adding a playful note to an elegant piece. The armchairs are covered in tactile velvet.*

off-white, or choose a fabric in a dark accent colour. Breaking up a pastel room with pops of bolder tones is an effective way to make the palette appear less precious.

Sofas and armchairs are essential elements of a relaxing space, of course, but you may want some incidental items as well. Coffee tables and consoles, poufs, screens, chests and bookcases all have a place in this room. Wooden pieces can be painted to harmonize with the prevailing scheme or kept white for gentle contrast. For added vigour, mix clashing colours. A footstool upholstered in a saturated tone could have its wooden legs painted in a pastel version of the same shade. These small details won't overpower the room, but they will certainly create pockets of interest.

Have fun playing around with your collections and rearranging them as you add new finds. Group artwork according to colour, subject or size for a display across one wall, or hang a single large painting. You can also experiment with frames. Black frames against a pink wall, for example, will strike a serious note amid all that candy colour. A mirror creates a bright punctuation mark on a

soft pastel wall. Similarly, witty additions that seem to be the very opposite of pretty pastel style, such as a vintage lampshade in orange fabric or a string of metallic bunting, will keep a predominantly pastel scheme light on its feet and full of surprises.

Collections of knick-knacks or china can bring little splashes of colour and interest to your living room. They may pick up and run with the pastel scheme already used – think delicate bone china in greens and pinks in a vintage pastel room – or they may strike the one pastel note in a largely neutral room.

Flea markets, garage sales and yard sales are wonderful hunting grounds, with the added surprise factor, too – you never know what you may find. Or simply look at what you already own. Comb through your belongings and find objects that complement the room, then have fun displaying them in pretty, original groupings.

ABOVE *Pastels, even when used in moderation, do much to soften an understated room. Pink tones on artwork, ceramics, throws and fresh flowers add hints of interest and help to break up large expanses of white wall.*

RIGHT *Installing decorative lighting is a good way to create visual interest at ceiling height. In this grand living space, a beautiful pink glass chandelier sets off the moulded plaster ceiling rose and ties in with the pink walls beyond.*

OPPOSITE *A glass vase is the classic vessel for flowers, but this picture shows how using patterned cups and ceramic vases adds an extra shot of complementary colour to a simple display – in this case, three hydrangeas in soft shades.*

Sleeping and Bathing

Strong colours and crisp whites can be too invigorating for a sleeping space, but pretty pastels, with their soft tones, create the perfect soothing atmosphere. Try out mellow hues in a bathroom, too. They bring playfulness to this functional space while gently warming up a white suite and cool tiles.

Televisions and computers in our bedrooms can inhibit our ability to sleep soundly – and so can strong colours. Not surprisingly, bright yellow and livid red are not conducive to sleep, whereas it is relatively easy to nod off in a room where soft lavender or mellow cream predominates. So, when decorating your sleeping space, choose colours from the pastel palette and you can't go wrong. Enjoy experimenting with shades that you might not use anywhere else and apply them with confidence, safe in the knowledge that they will introduce personality and warmth but won't keep you up all night.

When thinking about colours, remember that we tend to use the bedroom at extreme ends of the day and consequently view it in very different lights. On a summer's morning it may be flooded with sunshine, but in the winter or at bedtime we rely on electrical light to navigate our sleeping space. This has an effect on the colours we use. Regular energy-saving bulbs produce a soft, yellowish light that tends to make pastels appear warmer and deeper – no bad thing in a room designed for sleep – but, if you use your bedroom on and off in the day for activities such as reading, decorate it with a pastel a few shades paler than you would otherwise, so that it won't look heavy in broad daylight.

RIGHT *Bedrooms are often home to books and many come with pastel jackets. Find your favourite candy-coloured editions and display them flanked by fresh flowers.*

ABOVE *Soft grey and white make an understated but complementary backdrop to splashes of pastel here, while vintage mirrors hung together create a decorative display that does not detract from the restful atmosphere.*

RIGHT *Rather than sticking to a bright, white scheme, this romantic bedroom incorporates a few pastel touches. Used minimally, pastels can subtly feminize and warm up a space without standing out as its defining colour scheme.*

ABOVE *Two contrasting shades of pink have been used on this cupboard, helping to pick out details such as the beading and drawers and create welcome contrast, too. Ceramic knobs add delicate detail.*

ABOVE RIGHT *This crystal chandelier looks impossibly romantic with fresh flowers in soft pastel shades tucked in between its drops – the perfect look for a dreamy bedroom.*

OPPOSITE *This inviting, cheerful sleeping space is bedecked with pretty pastels and patterns. Confident layering is the key to its success. A patchwork quilt sits alongside patterned sheets and colourful cushions, and bunting made from scraps of paper and fabric playfully frames the scene.*

Painting walls a soft pastel colour creates a cocoon-like feel that is ideal in a bedroom. Carry the same paint across all four walls and even onto the ceiling for a sense of envelopment. To add character to a featureless boxy room, consider fitting tongue-and-groove panelling, available from DIY warehouses or specialist suppliers. Use it as a border running around the room and extending to half the height of the wall. With the bed pushed against it, the panelling will also serve as a headboard. Paint it the same pastel shade as the wall above, or use a different shade for a two-tone effect.

Patterned wallpaper has long been used in bedroom interiors, with florals being a favourite that strike the right note of prettiness and femininity. Stick to small, subtle designs that lightly pepper your walls with pastel notes. Think appealing backdrop rather than eye-catching statement. Or combine paint and paper for a layered effect that keeps your sleep space looking interesting but not taxing.

This bedroom is decorated almost entirely in pink, yet there is nothing girlie about it. The panelled wooden walls and a bedspread in gently creased linen add texture and character, while simple details like a plain roller-blind and discreet wall lights keep the space feeling grown-up.

Sleeping spaces experience little traffic, and we are generally not wearing shoes when we do use these rooms, so they offer the opportunity to indulge in luxurious textiles and textures at floor level. Lay deep-pile carpet that will feel fabulous under bare feet, or scatter fluffy sheepskins dyed soft colours across a wooden floor. If you put a sheepskin by your bed, it will be first thing your toes touch each day.

After the walls and flooring, the bed is another large component of a sleeping space, so it can really influence the style of the room. In an understated, neutral scheme, some pastel bedding will subtly introduce colour without spoiling the sense of serenity and calm. The addition of a dusty-pink throw or a lavender blanket to existing cream and biscuit shades brings visual interest but doesn't disrupt the pared-back look. Where lots of pastel colour has been used on the walls, take the opposite approach and opt for easy-to-live-with white bedding.

ABOVE *Floral patterns in pastel blues transform a simple bed into a cosy corner. A length of patterned wallpaper has been hung loosely, rather than pasted to the wall, and contrasts with a neighbouring yellow wall.*

ABOVE LEFT *The position of an attic room, tucked into the eaves of a house, contributes to its sense of cosiness. Here, a mishmash of quilts and cushions in contrasting vintage patterns makes this bedroom look inviting.*

RIGHT *A mix of fabrics in blues and lilacs is a pretty alternative to matching bed linen.*

Alternatively, adopt a mix-and-match approach, layering different duvet covers, sheets, pillowcases and quilts in pretty pastels and patterns. Scour eBay or markets for retro sheets with funky floral repeats, or visit any department store for plain, softly coloured bed linen. For a vintage cottage-style vibe, look for old eiderdowns, often made in soft apricot and sage, patchwork quilts and crocheted blankets. As long as the pieces have similar colours and patterns, the combination will work.

When it comes to bedroom furniture, most of us have a chest of drawers and a closet in our sleeping spaces for handy clothes storage. Paint a wooden armoire in the tone of your choice for a confidently pastel scheme, or leave the wood untreated for a lower-key effect. Look out for new or salvaged French or Scandinavian furniture, which often comes ready painted in harmonious creams, whites and sage greens.

ABOVE *Pretty dresses and a beaded handbag hung from closet doors become flexible artworks in a bedroom and add texture to a plain wall. This is a great way to enjoy favourite items of clothing, especially those not worn often.*

LEFT *This space adopts the less-is-more approach to decorating with pastels. Classic white bed linen, a timeless choice for any bedroom, is softly punctuated with a pretty patterned cushion in coral and butter tones.*

RIGHT *This handsome armoire gains a touch of personality thanks to paintwork in a very soft blue – a wonderful illustration of how pastels can stealthily bring colour to a scheme without dominating it.*

MONDAY'S CHILD IS FAIR OF FACE TUESDAY'S CHILD IS FULL OF GRACE
VAN WIE MOET DAT DAN ????

ABOVE *A simple display of cottage-garden blooms suits this informal pastel scheme, in which floral bunting and patchwork curtains feature. A pistachio-green ceramic jug and an old jam jar are the ideal vessels.*

ABOVE *Instead of hanging pretty garments from a cupboard door, here, a lacy top on a simple wire hanger is fixed to the wall with bright pink tape. The sign is a further quirky ingredient.*

LEFT *Deeply gathered curtains add a luxurious touch to a bedroom while also performing a practical role. Lined or thick curtains are vital for keeping out bright morning sun and providing privacy, too.*

Many of the pieces that naturally belong in a bedroom, from clothes to handbags, can also contribute to its atmosphere of pastel prettiness. Rather than stashing your jewellery, scarves and shoes in boxes and drawers, display a few of your favourites. The aim is to pepper your space with shots of detail, not piles of clutter that will get in your way, so be selective. Suspend necklaces on a row of hooks or from the edge of a mirror. Hang a sequined or embroidered evening bag on a drawer or door knob. Or simply store a selection of your most beautiful pastel robes and dresses on a rail so that you can enjoy their colours when not wearing them.

Unlike the bedroom, the bathroom is often used by the whole family and needs to perform a variety of tasks. It plays host to noisy children's bath times and hurried morning teeth-brushing; it is somewhere for a quick morning shower or a leisurely soak last thing at night. Most modern bathrooms share one thing, however – the

Dusky pink, seen here in the wall and bedside unit, works well in a bedroom, creating a soothing atmosphere. This space also makes good use of contrasting tones, including charcoal grey and neon pink, to stop the background looking heavy or dull.

There is an old-fashioned feel to this bathroom. A roll-top bathtub, raised toilet cistern and chunky radiator are all original pieces, beautifully complemented by woodwork in soft pink and antique lace at the window.

style of sanitaryware. The days when avocado or primrose-yellow bathroom suites were regarded as the last word in bathing chic have long since passed. Today, most of us have a simple white suite. White says clean, hygienic and fresh, and is a good backdrop against which interesting materials and finishes can be introduced, from limestone and wood to colourful ceramic tiles. It is also an excellent partner for pastels.

Pastels are not commonly associated with bathrooms, which are frequently small, functional spaces. In fact, we sometimes overlook their potential for looking decorative, but pastel tones can

ABOVE *While tiles and walls are regulation white, the small amount of woodwork in this bathroom has been painted in pastel colours – pink door surround, green cupboard – to banish any hint of austerity.*

Bathrooms are both practical spaces and quiet retreats, where we can enjoy a long soak or shower. In this case, fresh flowers brilliantly help to bridge this gap between functionality and indulgence.

LEFT *Pretty pastel style is nothing if not economical. Here, an old jam jar is used as a vase, with the label left on. At the window, a simple white curtain has been brightened with a pom-pom trim.*

really work in a bathing space, adding personality and warming up the space. This is especially advantageous in a room that receives little or no natural light. Try painting walls in a soft, pale pastel, but – bearing in mind the high moisture content in this room – pick a shade from a range designed specifically for bathrooms. You can also introduce colour by creating a tiled splashback or shower surround, or by simply hanging a pretty shower curtain.

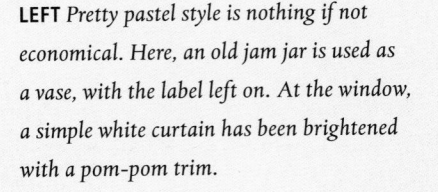

In a large bathroom, revisit the 1970s love affair with coloured sanitaryware and invest in the latest stylish interpretation of it – a roll-top bathtub with a painted underside. Choose between a reconditioned original and a cheaper acrylic version. You should be able to find a new roll-top that you can paint yourself, or check out large salvage yards for a restored cast-iron piece. Cast-iron tubs can be extremely heavy, though, so check with a builder or structural engineer that your bathroom floor can support a giant tub before you hand over your credit card. Finally, think about how you can use accessories to introduce pastel accents. Coloured towels and bathmats, pretty soaps displayed in a glass bowl, a painted wooden cabinet for storing bathroom essentials or a colourful blind at the window will brighten up even a plain white scheme, spreading pretty pastel style to the wettest room in the house.

A handsome roll-top bathtub, made from cast iron and complete withclaw feet, is a wonderful place for a soak. Its underside has been painted and then sanded down to create a distressed finish with notes of cream and green.

BELOW LEFT *Displayed decoratively, even the most unglamorous ingredients of a bathroom can look pretty. Rolls of toilet paper traditionally come in pastels, from peach to pink, and are here jumbled up for a pretty mix of colours.*

Children's Spaces

Decorating a child's room offers an opportunity for expressive design, but the room should harmonize with the rest the house, so don't succumb to cliché. Stick to pretty pastel style here, to pick out detail and introduce cheerful colour and pattern.

Pastels and children's rooms have had a long relationship. These colours possess a softness and sense of fun that is perfect for a young person's space. All pastels work well in children's rooms, but convention dictates that pink is for girls and blue for boys. We dress babies accordingly and we decorate their infant bedrooms in these gender-specific shades. Our young children recognize these colours as relating to their lives and interests, and go on to request them in anything from pencil cases to bedding.

This strict association is a comparatively recent creation, though. From the start of the 20th century up until the 1940s, pink was for boys, not girls, thanks to its link with red, a masculine shade. Blue, thought of as more delicate, was the preferred colour for little girls. Since then, the convention has been inverted, but this small story in the history of colour demonstrates how much fashion and social beliefs can influence the way we dress ourselves and decorate our homes. This is

RIGHT *Painted furniture is perfect for a child's room because it can be easily redecorated in a different colour, to keep up with the young person's evolving tastes. Look out for interesting vintage pieces, packed with personality, such as this multi-drawer chest.*

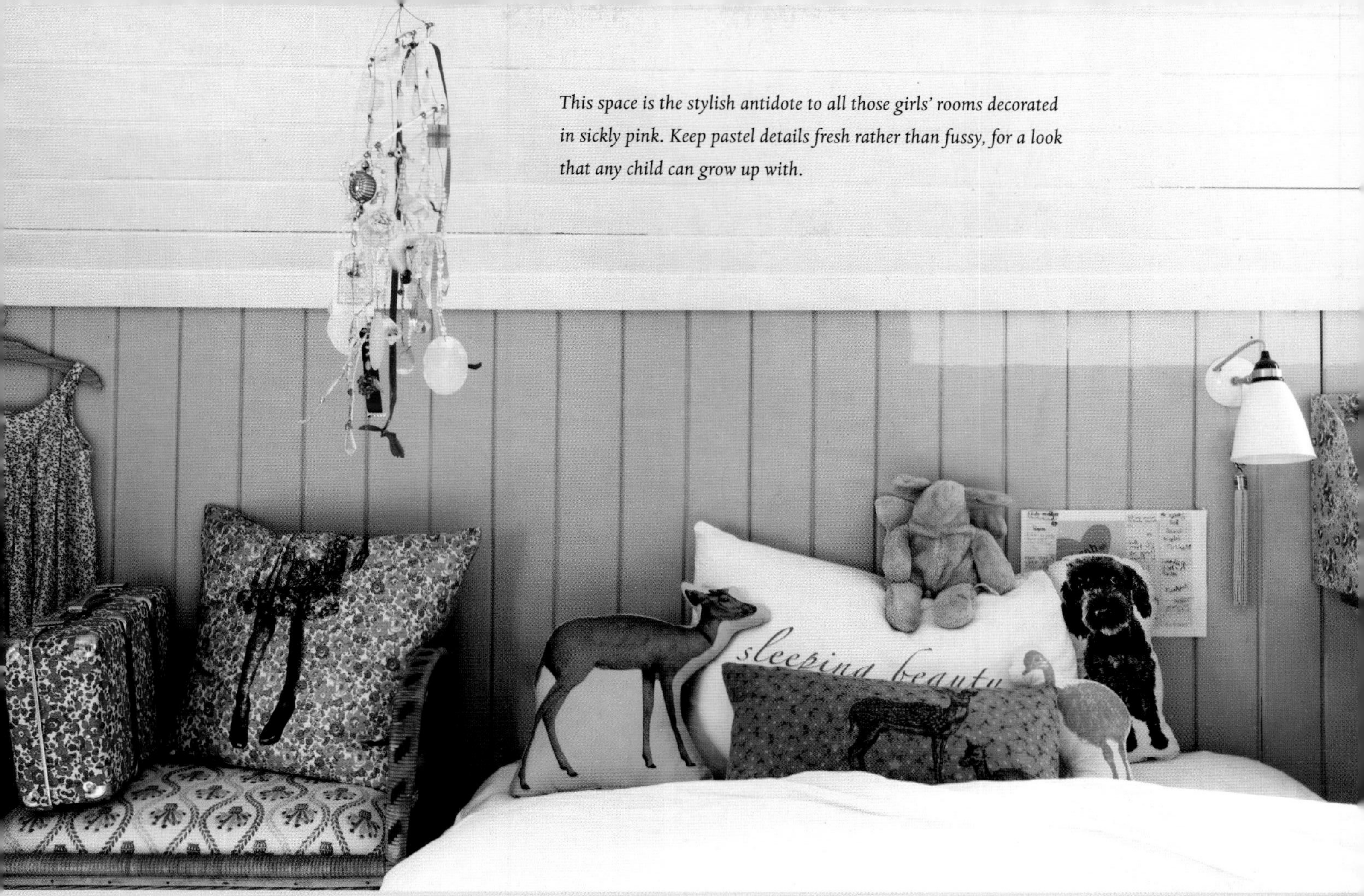

This space is the stylish antidote to all those girls' rooms decorated in sickly pink. Keep pastel details fresh rather than fussy, for a look that any child can grow up with.

OPPOSITE, TOP *Maps make excellent artwork for a child's room, being both colourful and informative. This vintage map of Europe has been teamed with a few decorative, quirky cushions and simple white bedding, to create a calm but characterful scheme.*

particularly relevant when decorating a child's space because children can passionately love a colour one minute, only to violently dislike it six months later. Many girls want pink bedrooms (and pink everything else) when they are at pre-school age, but often decide that pink is too 'young' a few years later – and demand a redesign.

One way of tackling this issue is to avoid classic pink and blue when decorating, and plunder the pastel spectrum for something similar but different. Lilac and lavender shades, particularly those with plenty of grey notes, are ideal for any child's room and more likely to offer longevity. Or go further off-pastel-piste and opt for pistachio green, cheerful yellow or soft peach – appealing to most children, but less closely associated with all things girlish or boyish.

Think carefully about colour right from the start. In a baby's room, it is the parent who designs the scheme but, unless you plan on redecorating the minute your child is old enough to express an opinion, make good use of neutrals. It's easy to over-decorate and create an extremely cute look for a nursery, complete with wall-to-wall pastels, but the design will have greater adaptability if you weave in plenty of off-white surfaces. The trick, as with any space in your home, is to build up colour carefully.

In this largely neutral space, a soft pink cushion and pretty pastel pom-poms are combined with hot-pink accents, via a pretty bird sticker and a felt table mat shaped like a rabbit and reinvented as an artwork.

In other rooms, this is simply a matter of playing safe, but in a child's room it's more about creating a scheme that will evolve not just with your child's tastes but with his or her needs.

A baby's nursery, for example, needs only a cot, some storage and perhaps a chair for bedtime stories or feeds, but a growing child may require all kinds of additional furniture, from desks and reading lights to wardrobes and toy chests. You have no idea what style or shade of furniture you may end up buying in several years' time but, if your child's room features a gentle pastel scheme that matches the rest of the house, existing pieces in other rooms will look right if you want to move them into it, and you will be practised at sourcing items that work with your 'look'.

As your daughter or son gets older and starts requesting colours for her or his room, add them in the form of bold pastel accents. There is an abundance of child-friendly pieces that come in appealing pastel shades. Take your pick from peg rails, lampshades, patterned cushions and comfortable beanbags, clocks, book ends, stools and storage boxes. A lot of contemporary children's furniture comes in strong paint-box shades and a sprinkling of these items will rev up your pastel scheme, too.

Think about how your child will use this space. Children's bedrooms

Pink and little girls' rooms go together like peaches and cream, but, when tempered by cool grey, as here, pastel pinks can stand alongside quirky collections in zingy shades, for a fresh and funky feel.

multi-task as somewhere to sleep, read, play, hang out with friends and do homework or art projects. In a young child's room, much of this activity will take place at ground level, so find flooring that marries practicality with comfort. Wooden boards can be softened with rugs, but avoid natural coverings such as sisal, which are abrasive – no good for bare knees and hands. As for walls, a wipeable paint or vinyl wallpaper is easier to clean than emulsion.

You need not rely on the high street for children's furniture. Second-hand shops and eBay are great sources for characterful pieces that bring welcome edge to a pastel room. Old school furniture, such as desks with flip-up lids, lockers and stacking chairs, are good buys – or track down a vintage child's bed in wrought iron or painted wood, for some ageless style in an otherwise ever-changing room.

Think about storage, too. Children accumulate a lot of possessions, from books to toys to their latest craft creations. The most beautiful of these can be displayed on shelves, while the rest can be swept into large-scale storage. Wooden chests and old suitcases provide out-of-sight space for a jumble of toys. Baskets, tubs, buckets and trays are helpful and safe, too – no drawers or lids to trap little fingers.

ABOVE *This dusky-pink paint could look rather heavy and dark if used throughout the room, but when painted on just one wall it brings welcome warmth without sucking up too much natural light.*

RIGHT *Carefully cut from patterned vintage wallpaper, these large animal silhouettes take up a whole wall and are a creative alternative to wall stickers or framed artwork.*

OPPOSITE *These vintage tins are decorated with pirates, princes and Disney fairies, making them ideal for a child's room. They also introduce colour and make practical storage for rolls of craft paper and small toys. The pretty dress adds a further splash of pattern that contrasts with the chalky pink wall.*

Whatever storage and furniture you choose, make sure it's secure, to avoid accidents.

Think child-friendly, not childish. Rather than bedding with an ultra-pretty floral pattern, choose a pink gingham, spot or stripe design. The tone may be girlie, but the pattern is classic and adaptable. Paint second-hand wooden furniture for a shot of colour, which can be painted over if your child goes off that shade. Adorn a plain lampshade with a row of tassels or hang bunting, paper pom-poms or your child's paintings as inexpensive, easy-to-change decorations.

Finally, remember that no other room in the house is likely to be changed as often as your child's bedroom. Be ready to repaint or move furniture, rearrange beds, hang new artwork, and gradually replace childish play things with serious student kit. Children's spaces need to evolve with the children who use them.

ABOVE *This French bed was bought at an antiques market and reupholstered. The owner then designed the room around it, using a sophisticated shade of pink on the walls that her daughter could happily grow up with.*

LEFT *A day bed creates a comfortable corner in this bedroom, but also provides extra sleeping space when friends come to stay. Its grey waffle bedspread melts into the background beneath pretty pastel cushions and a gingham quilt.*

RIGHT *This adorable doll's house is a fine example of how to decorate your home in pastels. From the blue duvet to the gingham tablecloth and pastel bunting, it captures the look perfectly – in miniature.*

Creative Workspaces

Whether it occupies a creative corner or an entire room, a workspace needs to function efficiently. Good lighting, a well-organized desk and plenty of storage will make it easier to get any job done but, to guarantee cheerful productivity, add some pretty pastels to the scene.

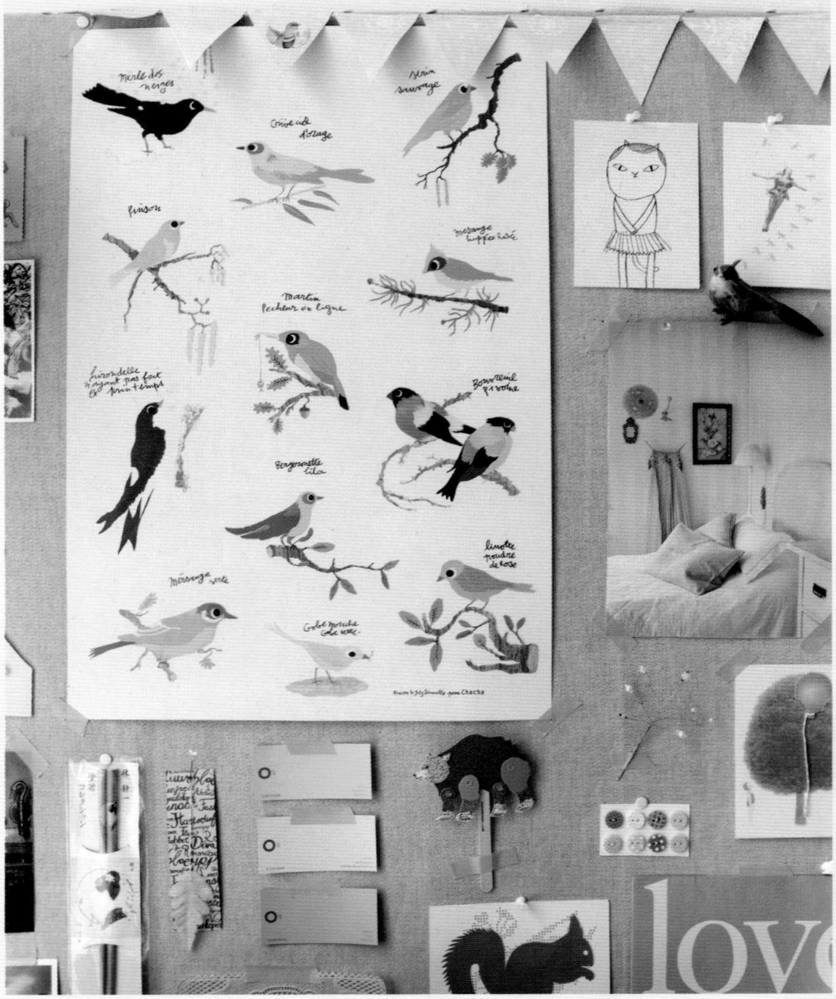

ABOVE *A simple fabric-covered board is home to an inspiring display. Pinboards like this can become cluttered, but here paint swatches, personal treasures and photos are arranged in an organized way so that each item has space to breathe.*

RIGHT *Feminine, ordered and calm, this is an appealing place to work. A lacy curtain and Philippe Starck Ghost Chair add an airy note to the pink scheme, while an unusual rotating rack – of the kind found in card shops – displays favourite postcards.*

Many corporate offices are shrines to greyness. Grey furniture and blinds and sensible grey carpet – it is all rather dispiriting, to say the least. Luckily, when you are decorating a workspace in your own home, you don't have to take design tips from the office manager. You are the office manager! So have fun and enjoy the freedom to create a truly inspiring space, whether you use it for nine-to-five graft or just the occasional craft project.

Colour can delight, soothe or invigorate, but it can also distract, so use it carefully in your workspace. You need enough to get your creative juices flowing, but not so much that the decorative scheme continually pulls your eye away from your work. Pattern, similarly, can be a distraction, particularly if you use a computer. Don't make a potentially eye-straining session in front of a screen even more exhausting by hanging hectic wallpaper behind your desk. A calm, unfussy backdrop is best.

ME
Creatief met blog

HAPPY VALENT NES DAY
BEST AUNTY
10 NEWS
One Trick B
be many hit wonders
JANOME

LEFT *An old table made from dark wood stands at the heart of this creative space, with a riot of pastel colours surrounding it. Fabric swatches await transformation into a patchwork quilt, while colourful, inspiring images line the wall above.*

RIGHT *This space has a long work station positioned by the window, where there is ample natural light to work by. An armchair and coffee table are the ideal place to retreat to for an inspiration break!*

Pretty pastel style, with its lively but measured use of soft colours, suits a workspace. A yellow- or apricot-toned off-white paint on all walls will create a cheerful atmosphere, putting you in a positive frame of mind and aiding productivity. Pink, meanwhile, is rarely used in public workspaces, so it's an ideal choice for a home office. A plain white room may appeal more – very sensible and uncluttered – but you can still humanize it with a few notes of lavender, mint or lilac, even if only on the desk legs or in a framed artwork.

The perfect workspace should look as good as the rest of your home, but be practical, ergonomic and functional, too. After all, you come here to get things done, so, no matter how large or small your space, plan it carefully. Think about who will be using it. Just you, or your family, too? Is it for work, personal admin, teenage study sessions or somewhere to sew? Is it part of

RIGHT *Decorated with a blue door and a cut-out of a bird, this simple cupboard takes on a new character. Its pastel colours are a fresh contrast to the wallpaper behind.*

FAR RIGHT *Practicality and good looks meet in this small collection of storage boxes and tins. They are perfect for holding creative kit, but look fun and colourful stacked together.*

LEFT *Bold wallpaper makes an eye-catching backdrop to this creative area. The desk is tidy and drawers provide handy storage, to keep the look striking but not chaotic.*

RIGHT *A creative space is often colourful because so many of the items used in it, from cotton and wool to coloured pencils, come in pretty tones.*

FAR RIGHT *Rolls of coloured tape and ribbon form a pleasing display on this pink-themed desk top. Even the scissors, with their cerise handles, contribute to the colour scheme.*

another room or a dedicated space? If you bear in mind the answers to all these questions, you will be better equipped to choose the right furniture and storage. Well-designed modern office furniture is abundantly available and can be quickly personalized by adding a patterned seat cushion here and some pastel stationery there. Alternatively, look out for vintage furniture. Snap up a solid old desk with drawers at either end, then team it with a wooden chair that you've painted a pastel shade. Old filing cabinets, plan chests and shelves are other useful additions.

Look out for pieces originally designed for different rooms, too. A chunky farmhouse table could make a good work station. Just check that it is high enough for you to sit at comfortably – kitchen tables can be lower than desks. Similarly, wardrobes, cupboards and dressers provide acres of storage for boxes and paperwork.

It is vital to be able to access equipment and files easily, but when you have finished working you should be able to tidy most of it away so that it doesn't become a constant presence in your life. This is particularly relevant if your workspace doesn't occupy a whole room, but instead takes up a corner of another, larger area. A creative space strewn with papers or half-finished projects can make a living room or bedroom feel messy and is an unwelcome reminder of work not yet completed.

Plenty of storage is vital and you should always overestimate the amount you will need. Small pieces that fit close to your desk keep equipment and materials conveniently to hand, without cluttering the worktop. Try a slim set of drawers or a storage box that slots under your desk and wire baskets or shelves, fitted to the wall behind the desk. In a multi-tasking room, clear a shelf in an existing cupboard for your craft materials or paperwork, or buy a big piece of storage that can meet all your needs in the space – storing work overspill and kitchen kit, or craft materials and DVDs, too!

Good lighting is crucial in even the most casual creative corner. Poor light can cause eye strain and, if the ambience is flat, it can make you less productive, too. Abundant natural light from windows rather than skylights is best, and if you sew or do other close work, try to position your desk near a window to make the most of this.

ABOVE RIGHT *This neat white space has been personalized by a sprinkling of pastel notes – on the chair legs, waste bin and stationery.*

RIGHT *Typewriters look charming, especially in a moody shade of grey. For a modern take, look out for a laptop in an appealing pastel colour.*

Situated along one wall of a living room, this creative space celebrates display, with everything from patterned storage boxes to pencils visible but neatly ordered. A backdrop of milky peach strikes a further creative note, suggesting that this is a place to enjoy crafts rather than to pursue a career.

LEFT *This cupboard is a shrine to all things pastel coloured and creative. Painted in a confident pink, its doors are hung with pastel fabric and its drawers stuffed with swatches.*

RIGHT *Pretty postcards and important addresses are stored in this simple alphabetized tray, which is kept on the desktop for convenience but also so that its colours can be enjoyed.*

BELOW RIGHT *The raw materials of a creative space, such as these balls of pastel-coloured wool, look lovely displayed on open shelves, tumbled into baskets or simply stacked neatly.*

General lighting, including wall uplighters, ceiling pendants and lamps, will provide a wash of light and reduce strong contrasts, but you will also need some task lighting for evening work or overcast days. A simple table lamp is not sufficient – the small pool of light it produces will not illuminate your work adequately. Instead, find a lamp with a pivotal head. Vintage lovers can buy reconditioned Anglepoise lamps on eBay, some of which have a clip-on design so that you can easily move them while keeping the work surface clear. A standard lamp with a directional head that you can stand next to your desk will do the job nicely, too.

The functional role of a workspace means it is often home to boring, uninspiring pieces of small-scale storage. If you don't have space to keep these office workhorses out of sight, you can still give them some pastel prettiness. Remember wallpapering your exercise books for school? Try the same idea on ring binders, storage boxes and files. Buy inexpensive cardboard office storage, then ransack your cupboards for wallpaper remnants, which you can stick all over them, or just on the spines, using PVA glue.

If your workspace is less about career and more about craft, have fun displaying your materials. Wool, cotton, ribbon, beads, buttons and fabric swatches are colourful and pretty, so don't hide them away. A simple shelf is a good starting point, on which smaller pieces like sequins or trimmings can be stored in old jam jars or decorative tins. Wool can be neatly stacked between bookends or

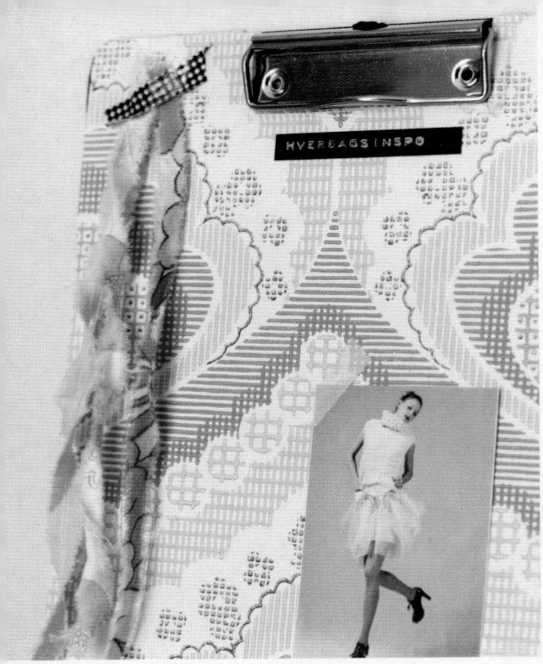

FAR LEFT *Pastels can find their way into a creative space in even the most insignificant items of stationery. Here, a clipboard is dressed in a funky pastel pattern and, propped against a wall, functions as a small noticeboard.*

LEFT *Pasting wallpaper to a no-frills chest of drawers, as here, instantly gives it a quirky new look. A lampshade frame has been covered in offcuts of fabric to become a piece of quirky art, waiting to be hung up.*

FAR LEFT *Rolls of retro wallpaper are a creative staple and can be used to cover anything from books to wooden furniture. Storing them upright in a container like this one is the best way to prevent them from unfurling.*

LEFT *Skinny strips of fabric in pretty pastel colours have been tied to the casing of this retro-style fan. Once it is switched on, they dance in the breeze and give this functional appliance a pretty, witty feel.*

thrown into a basket in a colourful jumble. Keep rolls of wallpaper or wrapping paper upright in tubs, baskets or even in an attractive wooden crate. This prevents them rolling open and looks good, too.

When buying even the tiniest piece of stationery for your workspace, keep your pastel goggles on. Why choose a sensible pencil when you can find one in pink? With spots on! And flowers! Shop around for these fun but essential bits of office kit. They make tiny colourful additions to even the most serious of creative spaces. Think sherbet-toned sticky notes or a waste bin woven from

RIGHT *Some people find lots of detail stimulating in a creative space, while others prefer it to look clean and uncluttered, as here. White walls and flooring are broken up with soft pastels on the furniture, but nowhere else.*

12
1
2
3
4
5
6
7
8
9
10
11

A wall covered with pretty images offers plenty of inspiration. Everything from patterned paper to photography and fresh flowers are displayed here, united by the same pastel colour scheme, for a relaxed but cohesive look.

RIGHT *Storage boxes have a practical role in a workspace but that doesn't mean they should look boring. These boxes in duck-egg blue with patterned lids provide useful storage yet look handsome stacked in a tower.*

BELOW RIGHT *There is nothing complicated or arty about keeping your pens in a cup – we've all been doing it for decades. But it is a great way to add a pretty pop of pastel to a desk top.*

coloured plastic; notebooks with pretty pastel jackets, or a cheerful mug that can serve as a pen tidy.

Create flexible artwork by taping up images or pegging postcards and photographs to a wire strung along the wall. This also becomes a great place to pin up reminders, invitations or 'to do' lists. Then why not forget the ergonomics and go for a luscious finishing touch with fresh flowers? Nothing takes the sting off a long day at your desk like a few pastel blooms next to your laptop. What could be better to gaze at while taking a screen break!

Outdoor Living

Creating a satisfying exterior space is as much about using interior-design ideas outdoors as it is about growing flowers. So approach your garden as you would any room. With thoughtful design and plenty of festive pastel style, it will become an invaluable place for both relaxation and entertainment.

You may have an established spacious garden or a bare courtyard. You may be redesigning your urban plot or simply brightening up your terrace. Whatever kind of space you have, and whatever its dimensions, apply the same principles and use the same pretty pastel style as you have indoors. If your interior style is minimal, go for a clean modern look outside with isolated pastel accents. If an eclectic look is more your thing, your garden may suit a less formal, more abundant design.

When your garden is directly adjacent to your home, perhaps with large glass doors offering views over it, it makes sense to link inside and out, to increase the feeling of seamless flow between the two areas. Splashes of pastel colour will create this link, but these need not be confined to the planting. Analyse your garden as you would any room,

ABOVE *This house is built into a hillside, with the decking at the rear jutting out over the garden. The white fencing and furniture look crisp against a backdrop of trees, while pastel pink on the garland, throw and cloth adds femininity.*

RIGHT *Roses in a rainbow of delicate pastel colours are cut and piled into a green child's wheelbarrow before being transported indoors and arranged. Roses bring a touch of floral luxe to any room, and these are deliciously scented, too.*

LEFT A glass tea-light holder with a metal handle has been hung on this stake, which has a grooved top. It makes a perfect place to display freshly cut flowers.

FAR LEFT Roses bring lush pastel colour to an outdoor table. They are supplemented with the kind of frothy, delicate wild flowers that grow abundantly in any hedgerow.

BELOW LEFT Rather than ready-made seat cushions, these chunky benches are softened with quilts folded to fit. They bring welcome colour and pattern to the white furniture.

OPPOSITE Wooden shutters open to reveal the interior of a pretty garden hut, used by children for play and adults for quiet relaxation. It is decorated with wallpaper that sports a delicate bird design.

BELOW This outdoor living space has been designed along the same lines as an indoor one. Flexible seating is placed around coffee tables, creating a sociable hub, while cushions add comfort and colour.

looking at lighting, surfaces, colours and accessories. Slowly, you can build up a pretty pastel look using a mixture of permanent features, decorative details, flexible furniture and planting.

If you are completely overhauling your outside space, think carefully about how you plan to use it. Do you want somewhere to relax, space for children to play or a huge plot to grow vegetables in? Keep your expectations on the ground, too. There's no point building in a large-scale alfresco dining area if the weather in your part of the country throws up only the odd balmy evening each summer. Perhaps a portable, easy-to-store folding table and chairs would be a better option – something you can put up quickly when the sun comes out and pack away just as fast when it starts to rain.

Get to know your outside space. Are there issues with boundaries or privacy? Where does the sun fall and how much shade is there? Are there any features, such as trees or a terrace, that you need to work around? You should also think realistically about how much time you can spend on upkeep. If you are very busy and have limited gardening experience, sturdy plants, plenty of hard landscaping and a small area of lawn will offer a low-maintenance garden. Or be more adventurous and design plenty of beds so that you can experiment with

BREAD

LEFT *Mismatched dining chairs painted in pastel shades are arranged around a circular table and teamed with bunting and a floral cloth to create a charming eating space.*

RIGHT *Decorate your exterior space as you would your interior. Here, a thread of tiny stars in hot neon pink has been hung up to add a flash of colour.*

FAR RIGHT *An outdoor space can multi-task as somewhere to play, sunbathe, entertain and work. Good Wi-Fi connection and a well-charged laptop (in a pastel colour perhaps) are all you need.*

planting or cultivate fruit and vegetables. It's worth taking time at the planning stage – your efforts will be repaid. Unlike a kitchen or bathroom, a garden only improves with age.

Use paint to bring colour into your outdoor room, just as you would inside. There are masses of exterior shades to choose from. Greens complement the tones of nature, or let the open sky inspire you and choose grey-blues. Pale, light shades will help to boost brightness in a small garden and will prevent a north-facing space from looking dull. Try painting fencing in a bright shade or, in a large garden, paint a shed or storage cupboard to create a focal point. Permanent colour helps to keep the garden looking interesting when natural planting has died back in winter.

When it comes to furniture, built-in benches take up much less space than freestanding pieces and help to add structure in the garden. In addition, there is no need to find storage space for a permanent feature such as this. Benches can also be designed with flip-up seats so that tools and folding chairs can be stored inside. It may be hard to make these storage cavities watertight, though, so cushions and blankets should be kept indoors.

When there is no space for storage, invest in weatherproof furniture that can stay outside all year round. Teak is hard-wearing, but its dark colour will fade to a silvery finish if not treated annually with teak oil. Remember to buy only teak furniture made with wood from sustainable plantations. Alternatively, furnish your outside space with second-hand pieces picked up at markets. These can stand a little rough treatment and are inexpensive to replace when they become weather worn.

When storage space is tight, another solution is to use stackable and folding furniture that can be stashed indoors without taking up too much room. Many chairs

BELOW *This child-sized furniture occupies a corner devoted to kids' activities. Colourful cushions create a cheerful vibe, while a mini wheelbarrow and watering can allow little ones to develop green fingers.*

designed for outdoor use, such as the deckchair or the classic café chair, also fold up, or look out for stackable metal and plastic seating. Some tables can be collapsed, allowing you to store them flat against a house wall for the winter. Or simply use pieces that would normally live inside. Bamboo, rattan or Lloyd Loom chairs look effortlessly at home indoors or out, while wooden dining chairs, brightly painted, will bring pretty pastel style to a terrace.

Many gardens and terraces are home to potted plants – a simple, flexible way to bring colour to even the smallest outdoor space. Terracotta is a pot-plant staple, but glazed clay or ceramic pots will add colour and are often frost resistant, too, so they won't crack during cold winter weather. Try planting up recycled fruit crates, food cans or old metal buckets and troughs for a more vintage look. Pierce holes in the bottom if you can, so that the soil can drain. You could even use old china teacups or jugs, but pour in a layer of pebbles before adding the potting compost to aid drainage.

When it comes to setting the table for a sunny summer lunch, you may decide you don't want to take your best china outside. Instead, use plastic picnicware, available in many different colours,

ABOVE *This outdoor space, with its white furniture and a few fresh flowers, is the epitome of simplicity. Folding chairs can be neatly stored when not in use.*

ABOVE LEFT *This vintage-style blue bicycle was designed by Olympic cyclist Victoria Pendleton for a UK chain of bike stores. It looks striking against a green-painted shed.*

RIGHT *An old gypsy caravan, parked in a garden, is a handsome example of how pastel tones were enjoyed in the past and judged ideal colours with which to adorn our homes.*

LEFT *Pink roses climb up a simple white trellis. They add colour to a plain white wall and provide fresh blooms for indoor display.*

LEFT AND RIGHT *A romantic garden tepee has been constructed from three thick poles lashed together and draped with lengths of patterned fabric. Bunting made from old handkerchiefs has been tied on, too, and cushions dotted inside for comfortable, shady lounging.*

BELOW RIGHT *The wood panelling and shutters on the outside of this house are a soft green with veranda furniture painted a similar shade. A roof offers some shelter, but, to protect wooden pieces used outside, it is advisable to treat them with weatherproof paint.*

or simply amass a collection of china in various designs from markets and garage or yard sales. This is an inexpensive way to build up a mismatched service for outside, and it doesn't matter if you break a piece. While you're hunting for china, look out for enamelled metalware, too – the kind of sturdy outdoor mugs and plates beloved by campers are great for a garden.

Use textiles to bring further colour into your outdoor room. Dress the table as you would inside, using a pretty pastel cloth and napkins. Scatter patterned cushions over loungers or cover seat pads in water-resistant oilcloth, which comes in various shades and designs. If you plan to linger in your garden late into the evening, keep a basket of colourful blankets close to hand. In a sunny seating area, create some shade with a parasol in a jolly pattern. You can change the position of the parasol as the sun moves around the garden and it will collapse for easy storage.

Remember to have fun in your outside space, accessorizing it with plenty of pretty touches and details. Drape bunting across a house wall, thread fairy lights through tree branches or hang a mirror to bounce light around. Add flowers as the perfect table centrepiece. For a long-lasting display, use a potted plant such as a geranium. Or indulge in cut flowers, whether home-grown or bought from the local florist, and display them around the garden in pitchers, milk bottles or vases. You don't need to use your best roses either. When carefully arranged in a pretty vessel, even common plants like ivy or 'weeds' such as cow parsley will look attractive and round out your pretty pastel scheme perfectly.

Resources

SELINA LAKE
Stylist and interiors author
+44 (0)7971447785
www.selinalake.co.uk
www.selinalake.blogspot.com
Twitter @selinalake

STOCKISTS AND SUPPLIERS

LIBERTY
Regent Street
London, W1B 5AH
www.liberty.co.uk
Iconic London department store selling innovative and eclectic design, with a wonderful haberdashery department.

PIP STUDIO
www.pipstudio.com/en
Dutch designs with bird and floral motives; includes textiles, wallpaper, porcelain, stationery and towels.

ANTHROPOLOGIE
www.anthropologie.com
Unique ceramics and glassware with products sourced from around the world. Stores across the USA as well as stores and concessions in London, Manchester and Edinburgh, UK.

ZARA HOME
www.zarahome.com
Pretty bath towels, bed linen, cushions and tableware.

OLIVE & JOY
www.oliveandjoy.com
Online homeware store selling designer cushions, tea towels, furniture and more.

GREENGATE
www.greengate.dk
Danish homeware brand, quilts, cushions, ceramics etc.
UK stockist:
www.berryred.co.uk

WOOD & WOOL STOOL
www.woodwoolstool.com
Recycled wooden stools with handmade crochet covers, and other cool crochet bits and bobs.

HOUSE DOCTOR
www.housedoctor.dk
Accessories, furniture and textiles for every room

BLOOMINGVILLE
www.bloomingville.dk
Lovely designed pieces for your home

LISBETH DAHL
www.lisbethdahl.dk
Danish company selling pretty glassware, candles, cushions and accessories.

NICKY GRACE
GORGEOUS VINTAGE
www.etsy.com/shop/NickyGrace
Beautiful handmade cushions, quilts and decorative items in an array of pastel shades.

HALFORDS
www.halfords.com
Classic style bikes including ranges by Victoria Pendelton and Pashley, also great for pastel car spray paints and camping equipment.

DAVID AUSTIN ROSES
www.davidaustinroses.com
English garden roses available as plants and cut flowers

CHARLOTTE LOVE
www.charlottelove.bigcartel.com
Beautiful illustrated prints and cards, including Pretty Pastel floral garlands, ice cream cones and vintage bikes.

CASSIA BECK
www.etsy.com/shop/CassiaBeck
Seaside, fairground and nature photography prints with a dreamy pastel feel.

JOYHEY
www.joyhey.com
Pastel fine art photography

BEG BICYCLES
www.begbicycles.com
Beautifully hand built, classic bicycles and vintage inspired cycling accessories. Bicycles available in delicious Persephone pink and flirty 30's green shades.

CATH KIDSTON
www.cathkidston.co.uk
Vintage inspired homewares, clothing and fabrics with pastel shades and florals prints.

LAURA ASHLEY
www.lauraashley.com
Furniture, wallpaper, fabric and accessories.

VICKY TRAINOR'S THE VINTAGE DRAWER
www.thevintagedrawer.com
Vintage inspired handmade fabric collage pieces, re-loved, re-cycled, re-stitched, beautiful embroidered signs, stationery and homewares.

THE YVESTOWN SHOP
www.yvestown.com/shop
Lovely blog and shop run by lovely Yvonne. She sells pastel coloured yarns.

ROSEHIP
www.etsy.com/shop/rosehip
Stunning handmade floral pillowcases with crochet trims, available in a range of Pretty Pastel patterns and colours.

LOVE MAE
www.lovemae.com.au
Gorgeous reusable fabric wall stickers, available in sweet designs including rain clouds, pantry labels and sweet nothings. Also very cute children's bedding, dinnerware and the prettiest gift wrap.

NEST PRETTY THINGS
www.nestprettythings.com
Handmade jewellery and hair accessories with Pretty Pastel colours.

LADURÉE
www.laduree.fr
Iconic pastel macaroons from the luxury Parisian tea room

SHANNA MURRAY
www.shannamurray.com
Artist and illustrator who produces sweet garland design chalkboards.

URBAN OUTFITTERS
www.urbanoutfitters.com
Quirky home details and furnishings with stores throughout the US and Europe.

GERONIMO BALLOONS
www.geronimoballoons.com
An explosion of giant balloons, ribbons, hand-cut paper fringing and fancy frills, perfect for parties and celebrations. Based in Los Angeles.

LEIF
www.leifshop.com
Lovely online store stocking matte pastel porcelain, geometric print textiles, candy striped candles and cute wooden storage boxes.

CONFETTI SYSTEM
www.confettisystem.com
Beautiful handmade decorations made with pastel tissue paper, silks and metallic gold papers.

SUGAR PAPER
www.sugarpaper.com
Sweet stationary and art prints.

LITTLE JOY
www.littlejoydesigns.co.uk
Pretty Pastel gifts and a lovely website.

PASTEL PAINTS

DULUX
www.dulux.com
Pretty Pastel favourite colours – Green Parrot 5, Sweet Sundae 4 and Summer Medley 4.

VALSPAR
www.valsparpaint.com
Pretty Pastel favourite colours – Lemon Sorbet, Pink Ribbon, Retro Green and Bird Song Blue.

FARROW & BALL
www.farrow-ball.com
Pretty Pastel favourite colours – Middleton Pink, Blue Ground and Tunsgate Green

LITTLE GREENE
www.littlegreene.com
Pretty Pastel favourite colours – Whisper, Brighton, Chemise, Drizzle and Angie.

PLASTIKOTE
www.plasti-kote.com
A selection of spray paints which can be used to transform second-hand furniture pieces, frames and bedsteads. Pretty Pastel favourite shades are – Pistachio, Pink Burst and Lavender.

SELINA'S FAVOURITE PASTEL BLOGS

blog.fjeldborg.no
brightbazaar.blogspot.com
citrusandorange.blogspot.co.uk
designlovefest.com
dreamywhites.blogspot.co.uk
frydogdesign.blogspot.com
kristybee-kristybee.blogspot.com
meukisleuk.blogspot.co.uk
molliemakes.themakingspot.com/blog
oncewed.com
rosehip.typepad.com
ruffledblog.com
sassyfrasstudios.blogspot.co.uk
secretsofabutterfly.typepad.com
studioofmae.blogspot.com.au
stylemepretty.com
sukkertoyforoyet.blogspot.co.uk
toriejayne.blogspot.co.uk
yvestown.com
zilverblauw.nl

Picture Credits

All photographs by Cath Gratwicke.

Endpapers; 1 The home of the artist Lou Kenlock, Oxfordshire; **2** The home of Nicky Grace, of Vintage Fabric & Gorgeous Things www.etsy.com/shop/NickyGrace; **3** The home of the artist Lou Kenlock, Oxfordshire; **4 above left** The home of the artist Lou Kenlock, Oxfordshire; **4 above right** The Battery is available for hire for location photography; **4 below left** The home of the artist Lou Kenlock, Oxfordshire; **4 below right** The home of Jeanette Lunde www.byfryd.com; **5 above right** The home of Martine Buurman www.omstebeurt.nl; **5 above centre & above right** The home of Yvonne Eijkenduijn of www.yvestown.com in Belgium; **5 below left & below right** The family home of Iris of irideeen.blogspot.com; **5 below centre** The home of Anne Bjelke hapelbloggen.blogspot.no; **6 above** The Battery is available for hire for location photography; **6 below left** The home of the artist Lou Kenlock, Oxfordshire; **6 below right** The home of Nicky Grace, of Vintage Fabric & Gorgeous Things www.etsy.com/shop/NickyGrace; **8** The home of Yvonne Eijkenduijn of www.yvestown.com in Belgium; **9** The home of Jeanette Lunde www.byfryd.com; **10** The home of Ida Susanne Collier of sukkertoyforoyet.blogspot.no **11–13** The home of Anne Bjelke hapelbloggen.blogspot.no; **14 above** The home of Martine Buurman www.omstebeurt.nl; **14 below** The home of Anne Bjelke hapelbloggen.blogspot.no; **15–16** The home of the artist Lou Kenlock, Oxfordshire; **17** Sophie Conran's home in London; **18** The home of Åshild Moen-Arnesen in Norway www.prydelig.blogspot.com; **19** The Linen Shed, boutique B&B near Whitstable, Kent, UK www.linenshed.com; **20** The home of Hanne Borge in Norway; **21** The Linen Shed, boutique B&B near Whitstable, Kent, UK www.linenshed.com; **22 & 23 left** The home of Åshild Moen-Arnesen in Norway www.prydelig.blogspot.com; **23 above right** The home of the artist Lou Kenlock, Oxfordshire; **23 below right** The Linen Shed, boutique B&B near Whitstable, Kent, UK www.linenshed.com; **24** The home of Jeanette Lunde www.byfryd.com; **25** The Linen Shed, boutique B&B near Whitstable, Kent, UK www.linenshed.com; **26** The home of Martine Buurman www.omstebeurt.nl; **27** The home of Nicky Grace, of Vintage Fabric & Gorgeous Things www.etsy.com/shop/NickyGrace; **28 above** The home of Jeanette Lunde www.byfryd.com; **28 below** The family home of Iris of irideeen.blogspot.com; **29** The home of Martine Buurman www.omstebeurt.nl; **30** The home of Anne Bjelke hapelbloggen.blogspot.no; **31 above** The home of Åshild Moen-Arnesen in Norway www.prydelig.blogspot.com; **31 below left** The home of Yvonne Eijkenduijn of www.yvestown.com in Belgium; **32** The home of Åshild Moen-Arnesen in Norway www.prydelig.blogspot.com; **33 above** The home of Ida Susanne Collier of sukkertoyforoyet.blogspot.no; **33 below** The home of Martine Buurman www.omstebeurt.nl; **34** The family home of Iris of irideeen.blogspot.com; **35** The home of Anne Bjelke hapelbloggen.blogspot.no; **36** The home of Martine Buurman www.omstebeurt.nl; **37 above** The home of Jeanette Lunde www.byfryd.com; **37 below** The home of Åshild Moen-Arnesen in Norway www.prydelig.blogspot.com; **38** The family home of Iris of irideeen.blogspot.com; **39 above left** The home of Jeanette Lunde www.byfryd.com; **39 above right & below** The home of Åshild Moen-Arnesen in Norway www.prydelig.blogspot.com; **40** The home of Ida Susanne Collier of sukkertoyforoyet.blogspot.no; **41 above & below left** The home of Jeanette Lunde www.byfryd.com; **41 below right** The home of Anne Bjelke hapelbloggen.blogspot.no; **42–43** The home of Nicky Grace, of Vintage Fabric & Gorgeous Things www.etsy.com/shop/NickyGrace; **44 & 45 right** The home of Yvonne Eijkenduijn, of www.yvestown.com in Belgium; **45 left** The home of Nicky Grace, of Vintage Fabric & Gorgeous Things www.etsy.com/shop/NickyGrace; **46 & 47 left** The home of Nicky Grace, of Vintage Fabric & Gorgeous Things www.etsy.com/shop/NickyGrace; **47 above right** The home of Anne Bjelke hapelbloggen.blogspot.no; **47 below right** The home of Yvonne Eijkenduijn of www.yvestown.com in Belgium; **48 above** The home of Nicky Grace, of Vintage Fabric & Gorgeous Things www.etsy.com/shop/NickyGrace; **48 below** The home of Martine Buurman www.omstebeurt.nl; **49 left** The Linen Shed, boutique B&B near Whitstable, Kent, UK www.linenshed.com; **49 above right** The home of Jeanette Lunde www.byfryd.com; **49 below right** The home of Yvonne Eijkenduijn of www.yvestown.com in Belgium; **50 & 51 above** The home of Yvonne Eijkenduijn of www.yvestown.com in Belgium; **51 below** The Linen Shed, boutique B&B near Whitstable, Kent, UK www.linenshed.com; **52 left** The home of Yvonne Eijkenduijn of www.yvestown.com in Belgium; **52 right** The Linen Shed, boutique B&B near Whitstable, Kent, UK www.linenshed.com; **53–54** The home of Yvonne Eijkenduijn of www.yvestown.com in Belgium; **55 al** The Linen Shed, boutique B&B near Whitstable, Kent, UK www.linenshed.com; **55 above right & below left** The home of Hanne Borge in Norway; **55 below right** The home of Jeanette Lunde www.byfryd.com; **56** The home of Yvonne Eijkenduijn of www.yvestown.com in Belgium; **57** The Linen Shed, boutique B&B near Whitstable, Kent, UK www.linenshed.com; **58** The home of Anne Bjelke hapelbloggen.blogspot.no; **59 above** The home of Åshild Moen-Arnesen in Norway www.prydelig.blogspot.com; **59 below** The home of Hanne Borge in Norway; **60–61** The Battery is available for hire for location photography; **62** The Linen Shed, boutique B&B near Whitstable, Kent, UK www.linenshed.com; **63 left** The home of Jeanette Lunde www.byfryd.com; **63 right** The home of Nicky Grace, of Vintage Fabric & Gorgeous Things www.etsy.com/shop/NickyGrace; **64** The Battery is available for hire for location photography; **65** The home of Ida Susanne Collier of sukkertoyforoyet.blogspot.no; **66** The home of Yvonne Eijkenduijn of www.yvestown.com in Belgium; **67** The home of Ida Susanne Collier of sukkertoyforoyet.blogspot.no; **68** The Linen Shed, boutique B&B near Whitstable, Kent, UK www.linenshed.com; **69 left** The home of Yvonne Eijkenduijn of www.yvestown.com in Belgium; **69 above right** The home of Åshild Moen-Arnesen in Norway www.prydelig.blogspot.com; **69 below right** The home of Ida Susanne Collier of sukkertoyforoyet.blogspot.no; **70** The home of Nicky Grace, of Vintage Fabric & Gorgeous Things www.etsy.com/shop/NickyGrace; **71** The family home of Iris of irideeen.blogspot.com; **72 & 73 above right** The home of Anne Bjelke hapelbloggen.blogspot.no; **73 left** The home of Åshild Moen-Arnesen in Norway www.prydelig.blogspot.com; **73 below right** The home of Yvonne Eijkenduijn, of www.yvestown.com in Belgium; **74–75** The home of Jeanette Lunde www.byfryd.com; **76–79** The home of Yvonne Eijkenduijn, of www.yvestown.com in Belgium;

80–81 The home of Martine Buurman www.omstebeurt.nl; **81 right** The family home of Iris of irideeen.blogspot.com; **82 & 83 above right** The home of Nicky Grace, of Vintage Fabric & Gorgeous Things www.etsy.com/shop/NickyGrace; **83 below right** The home of Åshild Moen-Arnesen in Norway www.prydelig.blogspot.com; **84 & 85 right** The home of Ida Susanne Collier of sukkertoyforoyet.blogspot.no; **85 left** The Battery is available for hire for location photography; **86 & 87 above left** The home of Ida Susanne Collier of sukkertoyforoyet.blogspot.no; **87 below left** Sophie Conran's home in London; **87 right** The home of Anne Bjelke hapelbloggen.blogspot.no; **88 above left** The home of Yvonne Eijkenduijn of www.yvestown.com in Belgium; **88 below left** The home of Anne Bjelke hapelbloggen.blogspot.no; **88 right** The family home of Iris of irideeen.blogspot.com; **89 left** The Linen Shed, boutique B&B near Whitstable, Kent, UK www.linenshed.com; **89 right** The home of Ida Susanne Collier of sukkertoyforoyet.blogspot.no; **90–91** The Linen Shed, boutique B&B near Whitstable, Kent, UK www.linenshed.com; **92 left** The home of the artist Lou Kenlock, Oxfordshire; **92 right** The home of Jeanette Lunde www.byfryd.com; **92** The Linen Shed, boutique B&B near Whitstable, Kent, UK www.linenshed.com; **94–95** The home of the artist Lou Kenlock, Oxfordshire; **96–98** The home of Hanne Borge in Norway; **99 left** The Linen Shed, boutique B&B near Whitstable, Kent, UK www.linenshed.com; **99 right** The home of Hanne Borge in Norway; **100 left** The home of Anne Bjelke hapelbloggen.blogspot.no; **100 right** The family home of Iris of irideeen.blogspot.com; **101** The Battery is available for hire for location photography; **102–103** The Linen Shed, boutique B&B near Whitstable, Kent, UK www.linenshed.com; **104–105** Sophie Conran's home in London; **106 left** The home of Åshild Moen-Arnesen in Norway www.prydelig.blogspot.com; **106 right &107** The home of the artist Lou Kenlock, Oxfordshire; **108 above** The Linen Shed, boutique B&B near Whitstable, Kent, UK www.linenshed.com; **108 below** Sophie Conran's home in London; **109–110** Sophie Conran's home in London; **111** The home of Nicky Grace, of Vintage Fabric & Gorgeous Things www.etsy.com/shop/NickyGrace; **112** The home of Hanne Borge in Norway; **113 above left** The home of Ida Susanne Collier of sukkertoyforoyet.blogspot.no; **113 right** The home of Martine Buurman www.omstebeurt.nl; **114 left** Sophie Conran's home in London; **114 right** The home of Hanne Borge in Norway; **115** The home of Martine Buurman www.omstebeurt.nl; **116 above left** The family home of Iris of irideeen.blogspot.com; **116 above right** The home of Nicky Grace, of Vintage Fabric & Gorgeous Things www.etsy.com/shop/NickyGrace; **116 below left** Sophie Conran's home in London; **117** The family home of Iris of irideeen.blogspot.com; **118–119** The Linen Shed, boutique B&B near Whitstable, Kent, UK www.linenshed.com; **120 left** The home of the artist Lou Kenlock, Oxfordshire; **120 right** The Battery is available for hire for location photography; **121** The Linen Shed, boutique B&B near Whitstable, Kent, UK www.linenshed.com; **122–123** The home of Hanne Borge in Norway; **124–125** The family home of Iris of irideeen.blogspot.com; **126 above** The home of Anne Bjelke hapelbloggen.blogspot.no; **126 below** The family home of Iris of irideeen.blogspot.com; **127** The home of Anne Bjelke hapelbloggen.blogspot.no; **128** The home of Jeanette Lunde www.byfryd.com; **129 left** The home of the artist Lou Kenlock, Oxfordshire; **129 right** The home of Martine Buurman www.omstebeurt.nl; **130–131** The family home of Iris of irideeen.blogspot.com; **132** The home of Nicky Grace, of Vintage Fabric & Gorgeous Things www.etsy.com/shop/NickyGrace; **133** The home of Åshild Moen-Arnesen in Norway www.prydelig.blogspot.com; **134** The home of Martine Buurman www.omstebeurt.nl; **135 above & below left** The home of Martine Buurman www.omstebeurt.nl; **135 below right** The family home of Iris of irideeen.blogspot.com; **136 above** The home of Yvonne Eijkenduijn of www.yvestown.com in Belgium; **136 below** The family home of Iris of irideeen.blogspot.com; **137** The home of Martine Buurman www.omstebeurt.nl; **138–139** The home of Yvonne Eijkenduijn, of www.yvestown.com in Belgium; **140** The home of Ida Susanne Collier of sukkertoyforoyet.blogspot.no; **141** The home of Anne Bjelke hapelbloggen.blogspot.no; **142–143** The Battery is available for hire for location photography; **143 right** Sophie Conran's home in London; **144–145** The home of Jeanette Lunde www.byfryd.com; **146 above left & below** The home of Anne Bjelke hapelbloggen.blogspot.no; **146 above right** The home of Nicky Grace, of Vintage Fabric & Gorgeous Things www.etsy.com/shop/NickyGrace; **147** The home of Hanne Borge in Norway; **148** The home of Nicky Grace, of Vintage Fabric & Gorgeous Things www.etsy.com/shop/NickyGrace; **149 above left** The home of Hanne Borge in Norway; **149 above right** The home of Ida Susanne Collier of sukkertoyforoyet.blogspot.no; **149 below** The home of Anne Bjelke hapelbloggen.blogspot.no; **150 above left** The home of Nicky Grace, of Vintage Fabric & Gorgeous Things www.etsy.com/shop/NickyGrace; **150 above right** The home of Åshild Moen-Arnesen in Norway www.prydelig.blogspot.com; **150 below** The home of Anne Bjelke hapelbloggen.blogspot.no; **151** The Linen Shed, boutique B&B near Whitstable, Kent, UK www.linenshed.com; **151 & 152 above** The Battery is available for hire for location photography; **152 below** The Linen Shed, boutique B&B near Whitstable, Kent, UK www.linenshed.com; **154** The home of Anne Bjelke hapelbloggen.blogspot.no; **157** The home of Yvonne Eijkenduijn of www.yvestown.com in Belgium; **160** Sophie Conran's home in London.

Business Credits

KEY: *a*=above, *b*=below, *r*=right, *l*=left, *c*=centre.

ÅSHILD MOEN-ARNESEN
www.prydelig.blogspot.com
pages 18, 22, 23l, 31a, 32, 37b, 39ar, 39b, 59a, 69ar, 73l, 83br, 106l, 133, 150ar.

ANNE BJELKE
Hapel.no
www.13tretten.no
www.hapelbloggen.blogspot.no
pages 5bc, 11–13, 14b, 30, 35, 41br, 47ar, 58, 72, 73ar, 87r, 88bl, 100l, 126a, 127,141, 146al, 146b, 149b, 150b, 154.

HANNE BORGE
website store:
www.bolina.no
E: netshop@bolina.no
T: +47 4790 8740

Boutique:
Gaml Drammensvei 38
1369 Stabekk
Norway
T: +47 6753 6145
pages 20, 55ar, 55bl, 59b, 96–98, 99r, 112, 114r, 122–123, 147, 149al.

MARTINE BUURMAN
www.omstebeurt.nl
pages 5ar, 14a, 26, 29, 33b, 36, 48b, 80–81, 113r, 115, 129r, 134, 135a, 135bl, 137.

IDA SUSANNE COLLIER
www.sukkertoyforoyet.blogspot.no
pages 10, 33a, 40, 65, 67, 69br, 84, 85r, 86, 87al, 89r, 113al, 140, 149ar.

SOPHIE CONRAN
www.sophieconran.com
pages 17, 87bl, 104 – 105, 108b, 109–110, 114l, 116bl, 143r, 160.

IRIS VAN DRONINGEN
www.irideeen.blogspot.com
pages 5bl, 5br, 28b, 34, 38, 71, 81r, 88r, 100r, 116al, 117, 124–125, 126b, 130–131, 135br, 136b.

YVONNE EIJKENDUIJN
www.yvestown.com
and
www.yvestown.com/shop/
pages 5ac, 5br, 8, 31bl, 44, 45r, 47br, 49br, 50, 51a, 52l, 53–54, 56, 66, 69l, 73br, 76–79, 88al, 136a, 138–139, 157.

NICKY GRACE
www.etsy.com/shop/NickyGrace
http://nickygrace.co.uk
Vintage fabric and gorgeous things
pages 2, 6br, 27, 42–43, 45l, 46, 47l, 48a, 63r, 70, 82, 83r, 111, 116ar, 132, 146ar, 148, 150al.

LOU KENLOCK
E: loulouk2000@gmail.com
pages 1, 3, 4al, 4bl, 6bl, 15–16, 23ar, 92l, 94–95, 106r, 107, 120l, 129l.

JEANETTE LUNDE
www.byfryd.com
pages 4br, 9, 24, 28a, 37a, 39al, 41a, 41bl, 49ar, 55br, 63l, 74–75, 92r, 128, 144–145.

VICKI MILES
The Linen Shed, boutique B&B
www.linenshed.com
T: +44 (0)1227 752271
pages 19, 21, 23br, 25, 49l, 51b, 52r, 55al, 57, 62, 68, 89l, 90–91, 92, 99l, 102–103, 108a, 118–119, 121, 151, 152b.

Artist:
Susan Wild painted the trompe l'oile on the walls in the salon.
T: +44 (0)1227 752884

MARILYN PHIPPS
The Battery
E: marilyn@thebattery.info
pages 4ar, 6a, 60–61, 64, 85l, 101, 102r, 142–143, 151, 152a.

Index

Figures in *italics* indicate captions.

Acknowlegments

BIG thanks to Catherine Gratwicke for your stunning photography. It's been a pleasure to work with you on this book; I so enjoyed our fun trips to Whitstable, Holland, Belgium & Norway – even the train rides and late arrival to the B&B!

I would like to thank my publishers Ryland Peters & Small for once again commissioning my idea for a book, big thanks to the whole team involved with the production.

Massive thanks to all who welcomed Cath and me into your pretty pastel homes – you spoilt us with yummy handmade cakes, lovely lunches, iced coffee, toast, visits to Peaches and Egg (Piet Hien Eek) and Hema! And thanks to Charlotte Love for your styling assistance at the Battery.

To Joanna Simmons – a huge thank you for putting *Pretty Pastel Style* into perfect words.

THANK YOU also to all the lovely people who support me via your blogs, attending my events and collecting my books. I really, really enjoy meeting you and so appreciate your comments and likes on my blog, Facebook, Instagram and your sweet tweets on twitter! #prettypastelstyle

Finally thank you to all my family, especially Mum and Dad, I'm so grateful for your love and support, and to my wonderful husband, my Dave.

LoveLoveLove – Selina Lake